Evolving Em

How To Move Past Your Limitations And
Live A Fulfilling Life

By

Joseph Salinas

Table of Contents

Introduction

The word Empath is being used more and more often today in memes and articles about emotions and relationships and popular psychology.

Do you know what an Empath is? Do you suspect you may be an Empath but are not sure? Are you an Empath whom struggle with handling so much emotion and energy? Are there tried and tested solutions out there that can help the empath not only cope, but evolve and thrive?

In this guide, we unfold all the secrets to the world of the Empath and answers all your questions and more.

Written by an empath and highly experienced personal effectiveness coach, specializing in the psychology behind emotions and decisions, and how to live life to the fullest.

Explore the science behind it all, learn about the pros and cons of being an empath, the different types and how to handle all that input.

Learn how to use psychological models and tricks to ground yourself, and how to grow and evolve as an empath.

Learn how to step outside your comfort zone to live your best life

This guide will change your perspective forever. It will make you more self-aware, keep you grounded and knowledgeable in the ways of the empath. It will assist you in clearing out the emotional garbage and negative emotions surrounding you, save you from toxic personalities, emotional vampires and dark triad personalities. It will help you chart a path for yourself to evolve

Thousands of readers have been able to change the course of their lives by implementing these strategies, and so can you!

Start reclaiming your life and passions today - don't let another person tell you that you are 'too sensitive' or should 'develop a thicker skin'. Be done with chronic emotional exhaustion and toxic relationships for good!

Read it now to give you the emotional freedom you crave!

The Scientific Understanding Of Being An Empath

What Is Empathy?

According to the Dali Lama, "Empathy is the most precious human quality". Generally defined as the 'ability to understand and share another person's emotional state, it is a multidimensional construct, consisting of cognitive and emotional components' (1), as well as behavioral aspects.

Trying to understand another's perspective, and how their experiences, biases, personalities, priorities, and concerns have shaped their perspective, is the process of empathetic listening. It is more than just sympathy, which is the ability to support others with compassion.

Whilst the 'capacity to feel and share the emotions of others (2)' is the most frequently used definition of empathy in social-cognitive neurosciences, which basically means it is seen as an affective state, with emotional reactions, caused by emotional sharing, it is not strictly emotional.

A broader definition states that empathy is a feeling that "enables to access the embodied mind of others 'in their bodily and behavioral expressions', irrespective of the content (emotions, sensations, actions, etc.) of the others; lived experience (2)". Thus, recognizing:

- Higher-order cognitive functions that underpin self-other distinction
- Conflates sympathy and empathy, which
- Share basic processes, such as autonomic processes and feelings
- Share outcomes such as pro-social behavior and moral development

Differences Between Empathy And Sympathy

Empathy consists of 'feeling into', and sympathy 'feeling with' someone else. (3)

The feeling describes one's mental awareness of the physiological and bodily states and changes (4) triggered by the perception of others'

- motor,
- somatosensory,
- emotional,
- affective or
- intentional lived experience.

The difference between empathy and sympathy relies upon three key components of bodily self-consciousness:

- self-identification (the experience of owning a body),
- self-location (the experience of where I am in space) and
- first-person (ego-centered) perspective (the experience from where I perceive the world) (5).

These distinctions are important to understand how important the awareness of being outside the other person and having to reach him is as a prerequisite for empathy.

Empathy thus has three core components:

- disembodied self-location (enabling to mentally put oneself into the other's body)
- hetero-centered visuo-spatial perspective-taking (coding for the others' visuo-spatial perspective) and
- parallel coding of one's body position in space (ego-centered).

This enables *feeling, thinking and understanding* what the other (as other—not me) is feeling and thinking from his/her own viewpoint and lived experience.

Thus, 'feeling into someone else' requires a clear understanding and awareness of one's ipseity (self/individualism) so that the other appears in his/her alterity (6) (otherness).

Thirioux defined empathy then as:

"Empathy is the capacity to feel and understand the emotional, affective but also motor, somatosensory, or intentional experience of others and their associated mental state, while adopting the others' visuo-spatial perspective and psychological viewpoint and consciously maintaining self-other distinction." (7)

Why Is Empathy Important?

Empathy facilitates pro-social behavior, enables parental care and attachment, and plays a mitigating role in the inhibition of aggression.

Researchers such as Daniel Goleman (8) and others

have shown that emotional intelligence and empathetic ability (a key part of EQ) is far more important than intellectual ability in long term success.

A study by the Center for Creative Leadership on Empathy in the Workplace concluded that:

- Empathy is positively related to job performance.
- Empathy is more important to job performance in some cultures than others (9), placing an even greater value on empathy as a leadership skill.

With fifty percent of managers seen as poor performers, according to a Gentry poll, the development of appropriate leadership skills such as empathy is crucial.

In some professions, such as the caring professions (medical and nursing personnel), where connection and compassion are crucial to the well-being of patients, empathy is taught as a subject (10), and studies have shown that interventions can be successful in raising levels of empathy. (10) Dr. Helen Riess from Harvard Medical School states: "Empathy is undergoing a new evolution. In a global and interconnected culture, we can no longer afford to identify only with people who seem to be a part of our "tribe." As {we have} learned, our capacity for empathy is not just an innate trait—it is also a skill that we can learn and expand."

Therapeutic empathy is regarded as an essential component of communication in health care training and is now taught in many countries including the US, UK, and South Africa. (12)

A crucial aspect of therapeutic empathy is to hold on to self:

Empathy is openness to oneself (why do I feel odd about the way he is looking at me?) as well as openness to the other (why is he doing that?).

It is a form of knowledge but also a skill that can be practiced and mastered. It consists of observation, listening, introspection, and deliberation. This is repeated in cycles as required to come to a conclusion.

This cognitive process acknowledges competing interests in a *respectful nonjudgmental way*. 'Its manifestation is that of the provider being fully present but *without the emotional complications of concern or pity*." (13)

This implies showing high levels of cognitive empathy, as well as emotional empathy and empathic concern without resorting to absorbing their pain and emotions. Thus, empathy allows emotions to be managed in a socially positive way.

By this definition, it should protect health professionals against burnout, yet we have more than half of those surveyed reporting signs and symptoms of burnout, and it may be because they have not learnt how to manage empathic feelings.

Empathy levels differ between cultures – there is the old Native American proverb 'never judge a man until you have walked in his moccasins'. The higher the value placed on individualism in a society, the lower the general abilities to display empathy (14).

It is about more than just understanding the viewpoint of someone other than you, it is about the ability to communicate more effectively: understanding their models of the world, what matters to them, what words to use or avoid. (8)

Three Types Of Empathy

Daniel Goleman describes the 'empathy triad' as

three forms of attention in his book on attention (10):

Cognitive Empathy

A natural curiosity about another person's reality

- Ability to see the world through other's eyes
- Pick up cultural norms quickly
- 'Theory of Mind' or 'Mentalizing' are often used synonymously.
- People with strong cognitive empathy may engage in:
- Tactical/strategic empathy - the deliberate use of perspective taking to achieve certain ends (11)
- Fantasy – tendency to identify strongly with fictional characters
- Perspective-taking – spontaneously adopt other's psychological perspectives (11)

Emotional Empathy

- Feel what the other person does

- Instantaneous body-to-body connection
- Tuning into their feelings
- Pick up facial, verbal and non-verbal signs
- Depends on tuning into our own body's emotional signals, which mirror the other person's feelings
- Chemistry, sense of rapport, referred to as the 'we circuitry' or being in the 'bubble of we' by Daniel Siegal, UCLA psychiatrist.
- Watching others receive painful shocks showed clear activation in the same areas of the brain during brain scans, indicating a simulation of the other's experience.

Empathetic Caring

- Expressing caring about another person
- Possible to have both cognitive and emotional empathy but not express empathetic caring.
- Heart-to-heart connection
- Partakes of the brain's circuitry for parental love.

Somatic empathy refers to the physical reaction you feel when you empathize, probably due to the mirror neuron response in the somatic nervous system.

What Is An Empath?

Whilst there is a lot of controversy relating to the actual definition of an empath, a simple contemporary definition is that of being *hyper-empathetic*. There is no definitive research explaining why some people feel more strongly than others, however, there are several theories posited and empathy itself is the subject of many research endeavors in psychology, neurosciences, and philosophy.

Highly Sensitive individuals sometimes have a special ability to sense what people around them are thinking and feeling. Survivors of early childhood abuse or later traumas often develop hypervigilance, which is a state of 'always being ready for fight or flight' responses, but it does lead to being hyper-aware of the thoughts and feelings of those around you.

Psychologists often refer to someone that experiences a great deal of empathy as an empath, and in some spiritual circles, it has a deeper connotation of someone with psychic abilities in sensing the emotions of others. Some refer to sharing energy or absorbing energy on behalf of others.

If you viewed empathy as a spectrum, as it is not only one construct, but multiple levels, empaths would be on the higher end of the spectrum. They show enormous compassion for others, but easily get drained emotionally from just simply feeling too much.

Is It Genetics?

Understanding the science behind empathy, it is clear

genetics play some role in empathy and hyper-empathy or being an empath.

Specific genetic studies have pointed to the arousal of the amygdala when shown arousing images (13) in individuals with specific gene variants. Other variants pointed to the ability to read emotion, sensitivity to negative emotional information (13), level of social skills and self-esteem.

Many experiments have shown that empathy to some extent can be taught, and an understanding of epigenetics will clarify the changes environment and other influences can have on a person's genetic make-up.

Many believe that developmental and environmental influences play a major role in the development of empathy in children, such as relationships, parenting style, parent empathy, prior social experiences and how we learn to deal with aggression.

There is no definitive research that conclusively points to why some people are empaths and others not, but there are some studies that have pointed in specific directions, such as mirroring, dopamine sensitivity, personality type, and others.

'Could a greater miracle take place than for us to look through each other's eyes for an instant?'

Henry David Thoreau

Why Do Empaths Feel Things More Strongly Than Others?

Some Reasons For Empaths Feeling So Deeply

Emotional Contagion

Considered to be the initial proof that empaths do exist, emotional contagion is described as the phenomenon that individuals often feel and express the emotions of their companions (11). The Mexican Wave is a good example, or one baby triggering an avalanche of crying babies in a nursery. Empaths pick up extreme emotions very quickly, which will overwhelm the empath eventually, thus necessitating setting tight boundaries.

Increased Dopamine Sensitivity

Dopamine is a neurotransmitter associated with the pleasure response and sensitivity levels have a genetic link (12). Many empaths are also introverts and they have shown higher sensitivity to dopamine than extroverts, so will need less dopamine to feel happy.

Mimetic Desires And Mirror Neurons

Mirror neurons are brain cells involved in compassion (13) and allow us to mirror another's feelings, as described by Girard (14). It appears that the empath's mirror neurons are hyperactive.

Electromagnetic Fields

Judith Orloff, controversial researcher and author (15), states that the HeartMath Institute found electromagnetic fields generated by the heart and brain transmit people's thoughts and emotions, and claims that empaths have stronger responses to these, as well as those of the earth and sun.

Mirror-Touch Synesthesia

This relates to the amazing ability to pair two senses in the brain, for example hearing music when you look at a specific colour or to ascribe a taste to words.

It also explains the ability to feel another's pain or emotions (16).

Sensory And Affective Links

Some studies show modulation between the affective links between an empath and their subject, in as far as the brain structures activated by pain is concerned. Higher affective links with high state empathy scores resulted in increased pain perception (17).

Fear Factor

Abigail Marsh (18) recruited anonymous kidney donors (what she calls the care-based ultimate altruist) to test how they respond to other's emotions and found heightened amygdalae activity in their brains when shown fearful facial expressions (19). It can be argued that care-based altruists are highly empathetic, and she showed higher levels of humility in this group, however, her research was limited to the altruism factor.

Sensory Processing Disorder

Empaths often describe their experiences as very similar to having SPD, which is an interesting paradox, in that many people on the ASD spectrum (Autism) experiences Sensory Processing Disorder, yet they are supposedly low on the empathy scale (20). Studies have shown the type of stimuli to affect the secondary somatosensory cortex (SII) in that facial expressions of pain had higher reactions in neurotypicals, but no difference was shown with images of mangled limbs (21)

> "It Is Both A Blessing And A Curse To Feel Everything So Very Deeply."
>
> *David Jones*

Why Everyone Has Different Physical Tolerances

Different types of empaths have different ways of interacting with the world. Physical tolerance for socializing appears to be linked to different personality traits.

There are two brain regions – the medial prefrontal cortex and the temporoparietal junction – that is important for empathic processing. Increased brain activity in these two areas is associated with empathic accuracy, according to neuroimaging and behavioral research (31). They found this activity associated with two underlying facets of the personality dimensions Extraversion and Agreeableness.

The Big 5

Psychological, behavioral and neuropsychology researchers often refer to the 'Big 5', or the Five Factor Model to evaluate the core traits, or dimensions, of an individual's personality. Whilst many personality trait theories have been researched the FFM seems to produce the most consistent results across multiple cultures, and each of these domains represents a range between two extreme ends of the continuum, with most people lying somewhere in between the extremes (30). Big 5 tests are scored in percentages.

Most people display two to three or more of these traits, with one or two being more dominant.

These broad trait dimensions include:

Openness

This trait features characteristics such as imagination and insight.

- High - tend to have a broad range of interests, are more adventurous and creative. They are open to trying new things, focused on tackling new challenges, loves thinking about abstract concepts.

- Low - much more traditional, resist new ideas, struggle with abstract thinking, dislike change. They are not very imaginative and do not enjoy new things or experiences

Conscientiousness

This dimension features high levels of thoughtfulness, with good impulse control and goal-directed behaviors, individuals that are organized and mindful of details.

- High - Will spend time preparing, pay attention to details and finish important tasks right away. Enjoy having a set schedule
- Low - dislike structure and schedules, procrastinate on important tasks, not good at taking care of things and makes messes. Fail to return items where they belong, or to complete tasks they have responsibility for

Extraversion

Characterized by excitability, sociability, talkativeness, assertiveness, and high amounts of emotional expressiveness.

- High - outgoing and gain energy in social situations. Enjoy being the center of attention, like starting conversations, feel energized when around people and say things before thinking. Enjoy meeting new people, find it easy to make new friends and have a wide social circle

- Low – introverted, more reserved and expend energy in social settings. Dislike being the center of attention, prefer solitude and feel exhausted when they are required to socialise a lot. They hate small talk, find it difficult to start conversations and carefully think things through before they speak.

Agreeableness

Includes attributes such as trust, altruism, kindness, affection, and other prosocial behaviors.

- High - tend to be more cooperative. Feel empathy and concern for other people, have a great deal of interest in others, care about others and enjoy helping and contributing to the happiness of others.
- Low – tend to be more competitive and even manipulative. Take little interest in others, don't care about how other people feel and have little to no interest in other people's problems. Insult and belittle others.

Neuroticism

Neuroticism is a trait characterized by sadness, moodiness, and emotional instability.

Individuals who are high in this trait tend to those low in this trait

- High - experience dramatic mood swings, anxiety, irritability, and sadness. Worry about many different things and experience a lot of stress get upset easily.
- Low - Emotionally stable and resilient. Deal well with stress, do not worry too much and rarely feel sad or depressed.

Commonly used acronyms to remember the five traits are:

- OCEAN (openness, conscientiousness, extraversion, agreeableness, and neuroticism)
- CANOE (conscientiousness, agreeableness, neuroticism, openness, and extraversion)

Empaths typically score high on Agreeableness and lower on the Extraversion scales, however, some extraverts can be empaths too.

It is important to understand the difficulties with

physical limits when you are low on the Extraversion scale, i.e. an Introvert. Introverts have to find solitude and spend time in nature to recharge, their energies get depleted in social situations very quickly. And because they feel so deeply, and are intuitively attuned to other's feelings, they tend to take on much more emotional baggage and negative energy from others than their bodies can handle, leaving them exhausted, confused and disoriented from time to time.

We need to account for individual levels of empathy as well – it is not a single unipolar construct, but as we can see in the scales above, it is a set of constructs on a scale from high to low.

Individuals that are very high on the empathy scale, and very low on the extraversion scales, will have more severe challenges coping with the emotional, psychological and physical demands of being an empath, being available for people to spill their life stories to, being a good and caring friend, and often, in the work-place, being a caring colleague or caregiver.

'In essence, not every individual responds equally and uniformly the same to various circumstances.' (30)

We can measure levels of empathy with a variety of psychological tools developed over the years – psychological research on empathy has grown tremendously in the last few decades.

Many commonly available tools on the internet have no scientific backing to them and were designed to attract followers to blogs and social media. A crucial component of measuring empathy is to ascertain the maturity of the 'self-other' construct if it is to be useful.

These two of the better-known versions measure the

different aspects of empathy and is best applied in combination testing:

- The Empathic Concern scale - it assesses "other-oriented" feelings of sympathy and concern
- The Personal Distress scale – measures "self-oriented" feelings of personal anxiety and unease.

Combining these two scales helps to expand the narrow definition of empathy and will reveal those that may not be empathetic. (31)

Are You An Empath?

What Are The Characteristics Of An Empath?

Empaths are affected by other's energy and emotions and have an innate ability to perceive others, intuitively feeling what they feel, plan or think.

Empaths share many common traits, such as:

Highly Sensitive

Empaths are particularly highly sensitive individuals, whom can sense other's energy and emotions, without anything being communicated. This energy may be positive or negative.

Absorb Emotions

They act like human sponges that absorb other individuals' emotions, and carry their joys or sorrows with them. They feel their emotions as if it is their own. This may apply to someone close by or far away, that they have connected with.

Highly Intuitive

A very highly developed intuition is a trademark of the empath - they are highly intuitive about people's intentions and hidden agendas and will often detect a sense of unease when around someone that is masking.

They can also intuit when for instance a person is sad but presenting a gregarious and happy front in a social gathering.

At times their 'knowing' seems to be deeper than just intuition.

Greatest Friends

Empaths make excellent friends – you could not ask for anyone more loyal and caring. They will stick with you through trials and tribulations and defend your honor to the nth degree if needed.

They normally have small social groups with very special friends, but the more extravert could have larger social circles.

Great Listeners

Because they are such great listeners, empaths tend to draw people to them that needs to unburden themselves, and often end up with virtual strangers confessing their most intimate secrets to them.

Their friends value their listening skills and compassion. They excel in the healing and teaching professions.

Generous And Extremely Compassionate

Empaths are generous to a fault, with their attention,

their compassion, their big hearts and their ability to convey that they truly understand what you are saying or experiencing.

They are very warm and altruistic individuals and will endeavor to assistant anyone that requires their help, whether it is someone that is disadvantaged, in pain or ill, or being bullied or abused.

They are highly tolerant and understanding and will put up with much more unfair treatment than the average person.

It is because of this openness and willingness to serve and support that they are so easy to take advantage of.

Highly Tuned Senses

Empaths have highly tuned senses in that their five senses work overtime – they are extremely sensitive to sights, smells, light, sounds, tastes, and sensations. This serves as a gift when you are so aware of your surroundings and can appreciate them for making the world so much brighter, however, as always, too much can be debilitating.

At times this manifests as Sensory Processing Sensitivity and an overload of sensory signals may overstimulate them, create anxiety and confusion and lead the emotional exhaustion.

Others may present with Sensory Processing Disorder symptoms and become completely overwhelmed, leading to sensory meltdown.

Alone Time

Empaths, like most introverts, often need alone time, to recharge their batteries and replenish their resources. They often need to be replenished in nature and will benefit from outdoor activities, whether it be a sedate walk in the park, or a long hike, or simply putting your bare feet on the grass. Other times they will need to participate in water-related activities as they find that very soothing, such as a soak in the bath, a solitary swim or other watersports.

Avoid Big Crowds

Empaths will always avoid big crowds, all the shoving and pushing, smells and noise can become overwhelming very quickly. Even if they do engage, they will excuse themselves earlier than socially acceptable to find a quiet spot.

Easily Hurt

As empaths are most commonly introverted, but with huge hearts that give freely, it is very easy for them to have their feelings hurt – by unkind words, acts or omissions. They can be emotionally labile, for seemingly no reason, but it is because they are carrying such a heavy emotional and psychological load of other's baggage and karma.

They are not scared of intimate relationships but will approach them very differently to the average person. They can find intimate relationships intimidating and may be afraid of losing their identity.

Know If You Lie

Empaths have an uncanny ability to know if you lie to them or twist the truth to suit your agenda. They can sense dishonesty and discomfort or trying to hide something no matter how big or small the lie.

They can sense sarcasm and humor used as coping mechanisms to hide sadness or anger, they know when you are selfish, prejudiced, jealous, self-destructive, angry or trying to hide something.

Take On Other's Problems

As empaths will often take on other's problems as their own, no matter the consequences to their own priorities or health, they do from time to time become overwhelmed by negative or painful emotions such as anger or anxiety

They may at times feel like they are drowning in other's emotions and become emotionally exhausted easily.

When emotionally depleted they may suffer from physical and mental exhaustion.

Dark Triad

Empaths are often targeted by the dark triad personalities, especially narcissists. They may fall for their false-self presentation and be drawn into their web of deceit and manipulation, as their only wish is to heal the damaged soul presented to them.

Self-Care

Empaths are often extremely hard on themselves and find it difficult to set boundaries to help protect themselves from becoming depleted and stressed out.

They are typically not very good at emotional self-care and can easily become victims of emotional burnout.

Loved By All – Emotional Connections

Apart from being loved by friends for their gregarious warm natures, kids are naturally drawn to them and they typically have the ability to connect with animals at an emotional level.

Predict Events

Some empaths have the uncanny ability to predict certain events, without any prior or special knowledge about them.

In A Professional Capacity

In the workplace they (9):

- show interest in the needs, hopes, and dreams of other people
- are sensitive to signs of overwork in others
- are keen to assist those with personal problems
- convey compassion toward anyone who has suffered a personal loss.

Different Types Of Empaths

Most empaths lean more strongly towards one type however, there is often overlap and one type does not exclude the other. One can have affective and cognitive empathy and feel empathic caring, and in fact, people with all three abilities make excellent teachers, caregivers and leaders.

Physical

Physically receptive empaths will experience the physical sensations the person they are with is experiencing. If the person is ill, they will actually feel the physical pain that person is feeling.

Intuitive

Intuitive empaths can discern specific feelings and emotions surrounding a person or event very clearly, often talking about a 'sixth sense' or an intuition that something is not as stated, or that something will happen or go wrong. These intuitions can make them very anxious and stressed. They are exceptionally good at telling when people are lying or omitting details.

Emotional

Emotional empaths literally feel the emotions of the person they are connecting with, without that person saying anything at all. For example, if the person is sad, the empath will have a sense of immense sadness themselves.

If they can get the person to talk to them, the person will leave feeling much better, and the empath will be left holding all those negative and painful emotions.

The emotional empath is the most commonly found empath and is really the few types of empath rooted in science. Neuroscience recognizes cognitive and affective empathy.

Telepathic

These empaths may be able to discern the thoughts of another person, without any spoken communication between them. It is not always clear thoughts but only a sense of what is on their mind.

Mediums

Also known as spiritual empaths, they may feel a connection to other spiritual realms or the deceased, and they feel physical and emotional symptoms from this connection. Some even have a visual component.

Many believe that they can talk to ghosts, or it could be angels or archangels, or other beings that exist in the outside of this material world. They can feel their energy, sense them or even smell them.

The Native Americans refer to the Heyoka empath whom acts as a spiritual medium between physical and spiritual worlds. They often heal with humor and acts as a mirror to show others what they need to see.

Nature

Nature empaths can sense the energies of nature, in plants animals and in geomancy the earth. They can detect changes in nature and the effect it has on the world's nature. They know instinctively how to take care of nature, such as plants or animals.

All About Clairs

Claircognisance is often an extreme example of intuitive empaths and is sometimes referred to as 'psychics' in general discourse.

There has been no scientific proof of any clairvoyant abilities or traits, and many people have been conned by charlatans claiming to be clairvoyant or psychic. A cognitive empath with no emotional empathy could possibly participate in conning and deceitful behavior, an emotional empath would find that too painful to contemplate.

Exceptional observational skills (for example, such as found in the hyper vigilant) combined with extreme empathy may give the impression that a person can discern things the average person cannot. Very strong cognitive empathy will allow the person to tap into the other's personality and reasoning and understand their intent. The popular TV show The Mentalist is a great example of this ability.

How To Figure Out Which Type You Are

You may have recognized some of the traits described above in yourself. You may wonder, do I have cognitive empathy only or emotional, or am I perhaps a clair? So much of the explanations above resonate with me. How do you figure out which type you are?

There are numerous psychic empath tests available for free on the internet, the problem is to find which are actually reliable and which are just a light-hearted attempt at getting clicks and readers in this era of social media marketing.

Of course, the only reliable test of your empathy levels can be performed by a psychologist, preferably a neuropsychologist, whom will have a whole battery of tests available, but may rely on a particular sample from experience.

Becoming more self-aware is a good place to start:

- Keep a small journal on you, or use Notes on your smartphone
- Record every instance where you have strong feelings about another's energies.
- For example, you visit a friend, you feel their inner sadness, but they are chirpy and talkative.
- Make notes of your feelings, the exact circumstances of the meeting.
- Wait a few days and discuss it with your friend
- You may find they have had time to process some of that sadness and is now willing to talk about it.

- If you watch a speech or a person of interest, and you feel very strongly that the person is not saying what they really want to say, or that there is intent in their minds that is different to their words, make a note of the context, and your thoughts.

- Follow up to see if your feelings and intuition was correct.

- If you sense energies that you cannot explain and believe they are outside of this realm, make notes of what you sense, in as much detail as possible. Do some research about places where you sense this, to ascertain if there is merit to what you experienced.

- If you find that your empathetic feelings are seriously depleting your resources, or that it is threatening your health and wellbeing, make an appointment with a psychologist to get some clarity for yourself.

- Take care of yourself first and foremost.

Being An Empath

Empaths, Intuition And Extraordinary Perceptions

Dr. Judith Orloff, author of The Empath's Survival Guide, offers this short quiz (31) to evaluate whether or not you are an empath:

Ask yourself:

- Have I been labeled as "too emotional" or overly sensitive?
- If a friend is distraught, do I start feeling it too?
- Are my feelings easily hurt?
- Am I emotionally drained by crowds, require time alone to revive?
- Do my nerves get frayed by noise, smells, or excessive talk?
- Do I prefer taking my own car places so that I can leave when I please?
- Do I overeat to cope with emotional stress?
- Am I afraid of becoming engulfed by intimate relationships?

According to Dr. Orloff, "If you answer 'yes' to 1-3 of these questions, you're at least part empath. Responding 'yes' to more than three, indicates that you've found your emotional type."

This quiz is a very basic tool – if you look at the types of empaths and the exercises to determine what type of empath you may be, you will get a clearer picture.

Intuition plays a big role in the lives of empaths, and very often when that intuition is ignored or suppressed, they find themselves in difficult situations wishing they had paid heed to that nagging feeling.

Intuitive empaths often struggle with extraordinary perceptions, their spiritual connections, and what is sometimes referred to as second sight.

Whilst there is no scientific evidence of telepathy or clairvoyance, many intuitive empaths can testify to experiencing, for example, a searing pain in their chest, at the exact moment a loved one passed on in an accident on the other side of the world, when they have had no way of knowing that. Or suddenly waking up at night with a start, knowing full well that something bad happened to your child, without knowing what exactly, but then anxiously waiting for that terrible phone call.

Many of them will fight this extraordinary perception, refusing to talk about what they 'see' or experience, for fear of ridicule and being accused of 'attention-seeking' behavior.

Dr. Judith Orloff, author of several books on being an empath, and an Assistant Professor of Psychiatry, claims to have been born with 'second sight', and cutting-edge knowledge of intuition, energy, and spirituality. Her works have helped many empaths navigate their gifts in a way that promotes self-care and helped them understand why they feel so different, however, her writings on extraordinary perceptions have labeled her as very controversial and not 'scientific' in the academic community that she is supposed to be a member of.

The Gift Of Being An Empath

Being an empath is a gift. Empathy is a wonderful trait to have and will smooth personal interactions throughout your life, and tipping the higher end of the scale endows you with gifts not many people possess. They are open to physical, emotional and psychological information that is mostly inaccessible to the average person. These gifts are non-confrontational and can be used for the greater good and empaths should hone their skills in these gifts throughout life.

The gift of being an empath includes:

- They are naturally curious about everything around them, and when grounded and centered in themselves, will enjoy life to the fullest. They love to travel and meaningful experiences.

- They make the most wonderful, loyal friends, no one could ask for a greater gift than an empath friend. Their warmth and compassion touch the lives of all around them and leaves them feeling replete over the long term as their sense of purpose is fulfilled.

- They are great listeners, and will thus be privy to many great, deep and sad stories from all walks of life, giving reassurance to the storyteller that they are going to be fine no matter what happens.

- They are loved by children and animals and often form very strong emotional bonds with them, leading to a much enriched life. They love communing with nature and appreciates the gifts of life around them, every sunrise or flower or sunset, which assists with engendering mindfulness.

- They make strong leaders, great visionaries and can easily convince their followers to do the right thing, behave ethically and will often chart new courses and conquer new markets or ideas
- They have good working relationships due to their caring and compassionate natures, and their ability to understand other's points of view. This minimizes stress in the workplace.
- They adapt easily to working with or living in different cultures – Psychologists refer to a 'false consensus effect' (26) which basically means that because people are familiar with their own beliefs and opinions, they greatly overestimate the number of people that share them, which is an egocentric bias in social perception and attribution. This cognitive bias is due to the availability heuristic (what comes to mind quickly is seen as significant) and makes them blind to cultural differences, which can lead to misunderstandings, anger and negative discourse. Empaths, on the other hand, can pick up easily on cultural differences

and have an uncanny ability to understand different points of view and beliefs.

- They excel in the healing and teaching professions, as they have caring and nurturing natures

- They are very big-hearted people (but sometimes give too much), have passionate and deep relationships that are soul-satisfying and enriching

- Their highly tuned senses and intuition is great for negotiations or eliciting the truth from scared or traumatized people

- They are emotionally intelligent, a particularly valued skill in the competitive workplace today.

- They are dreamers and idealists that can see the big picture, even when paying attention to the detail of someone's story. They can be extremely creative, which lead to rich and fulfilling lives.

The Dark Side Of Being An Empath

Does empathy lead to compassion fatigue or satisfaction? It seems to be time-dependent, intense feelings have been linked to fatigue in the short term but to satisfaction in the long term (22) for most, for others, there have been correlations to burnout.

The ability to recognize another's perspective and thinking beyond yourself is a valuable attribute, however, for the empath, this may become toxic if not managed properly.

Some of the negative issues related to being an empath include:

Feeling Drained After Spending Time Around People

Empaths expend emotional energy to socialise, and especially introverted empaths will need to muster all they have to participate in social activities, make small talk and listen to people tell them far more than what is socially acceptable. They will often feel the need to leave social gatherings after a couple of hours, in order to find some solitude to unwind and recharge.

Confusing, Disorienting, Exhausting

When empaths are engaged in a lot of socialising over a period, with no break to recharge and work through the muddle of emotional and psychological baggage they have picked up along the way, it can easily leave an empath confused and disoriented. This is particularly true when the empath is not skilled in handling the incoming loads and does not have a clear sense of self-other.

They will wonder why they feel so exhausted, and sad maybe, especially if they do not intellectually believe they have something to feel sad about, not understanding that they have picked up the sadness and emotional pain from people they have been in contact with. They may wonder what is wrong with them, why they cannot shake those negative feelings when they have so much to be grateful for.

Feel Other's Physical Pain

Feeling others' physical pain can confound issues even more. Not all empaths will feel physical pain, but those who do can find it very disturbing to experience another's physical pain in their own bodies.

Hate Interpersonal Conflicts

Empaths hate interpersonal conflicts with a passion – it makes them extremely uncomfortable, to the point of experiencing anxiety and physical pain.

They will do anything to avoid interpersonal conflict, and this is often the reason for them 'giving in' to unreasonable demands on their time and energy, anything to avoid the inevitable unpleasantness if they do not.

Cannot Witness Violence Or Any Form Of Cruelty

Having to witness violence or any other form of cruelty can be extremely painful for the empath. They may show mimicry or emotional contagion

They will cover their eyes and ears, and experience high levels of anxiety. If reading a book, they will often cry, if watching a television series or a movie, they will show very strong visceral reactions and may get up and walk out to avoid being a witness.

As younger children, they will cry and run away if witnessing the schoolyard bully being mean and be traumatised by it.

Research has shown (36) that when giving subjects mild electrical shocks, individuals with high empathy levels will experience the same physical pain when watching it, and more so when it is a subject in a group they identify with.

Physical And Emotional Fatigue

Often suffer physical and emotional fatigue, can get weighed down by other's negative emotional energy so much so that it creates psychological disharmony.

Hangovers

They do not enjoy large crowds and can experience emotional and social hangovers. Introverts become overstimulated and exhausted a lot quicker than their counterparts.

Whilst they enjoy socialising as much as the average person, they approach it in a very different way, and will typically engage and talk to only a few people, but their conversations will be much deeper than banal small talk and gossiping. Empaths certainly do not lack the confidence to engage in social intercourse, and some actively seek out interesting debates on a wide range of topics, that will stimulate intellectual repartee and discourse.

It is in the pursuit of these deeper conversations that others will open up to the empath and share very personal and emotional stories with them, overloading them with negative and emotional baggage. Typically, the person they conversed with will feel much better after the conversation, as if they had a load lifted off their shoulders.

Sensory Overload

Empaths can easily become overwhelmed and overstimulated in noisy, crowded and busy areas due to Sensory Processing Sensitivity (SPS) and some may have Sensory Processing Disorder (SPD).

They may avoid big and loud gatherings, such as political rallies or music concerts, or any other noisy gathering. Even if they love music for example, and do attend a concert, they will feel the effects of sensory overload very quickly.

Sensory overload can be caused by a low threshold to stimulation from sound, light, smells, colours, touch (feeling crowded in) and incessant chatter or multiple conversations in the same room. When the five senses produce more inputs than the brain can handle and process at the same time, it may get 'stuck' trying to prioritise what to process first and will produce the symptoms of sensory overload.

Signs of sensory overload include:

- Extreme irritability
- Problems focusing due to competing inputs
- Discomfort and palpitations
- Restlessness and erratic movements
- Hyper-excitement and a feeling of being 'wound up' and off-balance

- Hyper-awareness of the environment and a feeling of needing to get out
- Stress, anxiety and even fear about your surroundings
- Closing your eyes, nose or even covering up your ears to stop the constant stream of inputs.
- Taking off items of clothing as they scratch or itch, even brushing or flossing your teeth hurts.
- Being revolted by anyone touching you, even if just a hand on your arm to calm you or stabilize you.
- Every sensory input is amplified into a cacophony of sounds, lights, smells, tastes and textures that becomes overwhelming and leaves you gasping for air.

Sensory overload builds up slowly but can quickly morph into a crescendo of sensual assaults if not dealt with timeously, by removing yourself from the situation and finding a calm place to recharge.

Linked To Social Anxiety

Empaths may be seen as suffering from social anxiety because they need to retreat and recharge so often, however, their motivation for shunning social contact for periods of time is very different to people with real social anxiety illness, which is mostly about fear of rejection as opposed to the empath's need to recharge their batteries so to speak in order to be available again for their social circle.

They can appear stand-offish or aloof, however, their aloofness is purely used as a protective device against inauthentic people. They can sense inauthenticity quicker than a dog can find a bone buried in the backyard, and once they have honed their personal protection skills, they will make an effort to avoid such people due to the chaos and problems they bring with them.

Isolated And Lonely

Empaths could become isolated and lonely, especially

if they give too much to close friend or intimate partner on an ongoing basis, which will leave them depleted, disoriented and less likely to socialise with a bigger circle of friends. They may also be deliberately isolated from family and friends by this person if there is underlying pathology.

Intimate Relationships

Empaths may become scared of intimate relationships and feel crowded very quickly. This is not based on fear of rejection as is commonly assumed, but rather on the overwhelming responsibility of taking on an intimate partner's happiness if there are no clear self-other boundaries in the relationship.

In addition, past mistakes in choosing an intimate partner, that turned out to be emotionally draining or abusive, may leave the empath with traces or scores of trust issues.

Often Need Time To Recharge

Empaths need time to recharge, often. This may conflict with busy schedules and daily demands on their time or other's expectations of their availability.

Other persons, whom may not know or understand the needs of the empath, may view this behaviour as erratic or being unreliable. They may see withdrawal periods as being anti-social, or depressed times. Inauthentic people will view their withdrawal from their incessant demands on their time and senses as being stuck-up or aloof.

However, if empaths do not recharge regularly, they will become overloaded, exhausted, confused and disoriented, and may start showing physical, emotional and psychological manifestations of long-term stress.

Selfish Friends

Because the empath is such a generous, loyal and caring friend, they open themselves up to being taken advantage of by the more selfish amongst their friends.

These spoiled, selfish individuals will quickly learn that the empath is always there for them, no matter time of day or whatever is going on in their own lives. They know, from experience, that the empath will drop whatever is happening at that moment to assist them, listen to them and empathise with their issues and problems.

Whilst it is the greatest gift to someone in real trouble, some friends will use their empath friend as a dumping ground for their emotional baggage and problems, acting as if it is their right to vent and dump whenever and oftentimes on a daily basis.

They leave the interaction feeling relieved of negative

energy, and validated, not even considering that the empath is holding all their negative energy and must try to make sense of it first before they can return to their own lives.

The friends are not malevolent, like energy vampires and dark triad personalities, they are just ignorant and selfish.

However, the constant dumping and emotional and psychological overload can leave the empath feeling drained, exhausted, depleted and may even present over the long term with depressive symptoms.

Emotional Vampires

Empaths and Highly Sensitive People (HSP's) easily fall victim to emotional vampires whom target them for their emotional strength.

It is a commonly used colloquial term for toxic

people, whom will drain the empath and leave them feeling completely exhausted. It was first termed by Albert Bernstein, Ph.D. in a book on the topic (35).

Whilst the term is often used to describe dark triad personalities, in this instance we are talking about toxic individuals that are simply self-absorbed, completely self-centred and whom will knowingly target others with warmth, compassion and healthy energy, to feed their own inner emptiness.

They include individuals that like to play the Victim, the Drama Queen, Constant Talkers (about themselves), the Antisocial (spurns social norms, reckless thrill seeker) and the Controlling personalities.

Emotional vampires lack three of the six pillars of self-esteem (35), as described by Mark Manson:

- Excessive need for validation or attention from others

- The belief that little to nothing is ever their fault
- The lack of self-awareness to recognize their self-defeating patterns

The danger here lies in the three traits reinforcing each other, and their ability to 'suck in and hurt good people' (36).

Emotional vampires are manipulative, jealous, lack empathy, have an excessive sense of entitlement and shows a blatant disregard for their effect on the empath's emotions.

They engage in extremely one-sided relationships, take whatever they can without blinking an eye, make decisions on your behalf without your consent and completely disregard your needs and wishes.

They create chaos wherever they go, will sabotage and undermine you at will, behave defensively and use projection extensively. It feels like they suck the air out of a room. Sadly, their negative influence can be felt long after they are gone.

Emotional vampires will dig at you with seemingly innocuous remarks (you're too sensitive) that eats away at your self-worth or deliver the jibe as a joke. The even more malignant dark triad personalities will make you seriously question your own worth.

They leave the empath feeling emotionally drained, exhausted, anxious, confused, frightened, emotionally unsafe, depressed and in pain. The empath may suddenly crave comfort foods and feel put down or dirtied.

They will affect the empath's ability to take care of themselves, their decision-making abilities as well as their physical, mental and emotional health.

Addictions

Sadly, empaths that have not learnt to take care of themselves may resort to addictions to numb their overloaded sensitivities, and engage in self-destructive behaviour such as overeating, alcohol, drugs and risky sexual endeavours.

Many empaths will overeat at times of stress or feeling threatened, in order to build up a symbolic protective layer around themselves.

Self-harming behaviour or attempted suicide is not common, but is possible, especially if there are underlying psychological and emotional issues.

Emotional Burnout

Emotional burnout occurs when an individual reaches a state of physical, mental and emotional exhaustion due to prolonged and ongoing stress. Initially, the term was used to describe emotional exhaustion in the health care professions, but it is now used for all stress related emotional exhaustion.

It leaves the individual feeling overwhelmed, completely drained emotionally and unable to meet demands made on them. They feel like they have nothing more to give, they are disengaged and detached, helpless, hopeless, defeated, cynical and very often extremely resentful. The overriding emotional exhaustion and cynicism are early tell-tale signs.

Eventually, emotional burnout will affect your ability to function and be a productive member of society and will cause long-term changes to your physical health.

Empaths that do not practice self-care are particularly vulnerable to emotional burnout, as are those in the midst of the emotional vortex that is a relationship with one of the dark triad personalities.

Whilst burnout is often the result of chronic and unrelenting stress, it is itself different from stress. Stress is always about 'too much' - too many physical, mental and emotional demands, whereas burnout is about 'not enough' – feeling emotionally drained and blunted, without motivation, mentally exhausted and dried up, feeling completely empty with nothing left to give.

The most commonly used burnout questionnaire is the Maslach Burnout Inventory Scale, administered by psychologists. (38) It measures subscales called Emotional Exhaustion, Depersonalisation, Cynicism, Personal Accomplishment and Involvement. If the first three measures high and the last two low, it points to burnout.

Narcissists And Other Dark Triad Personalities

Empaths are often targeted by dark triad personalities because of their giving natures and big hearts and may end up being severely abused, emotionally, mentally, physically, financially and sexually. They may even be induced into a life of crime on behalf of the abuser, even though they have no criminal inclinations themselves.

What are the dark triad personalities?

The dark triad (DT) traits include:

- Narcissism
- Machiavellianism
- Psychopathy

It is referred to as 'dark' because of their extremely malevolent qualities, and individuals with these traits are more likely to commit crimes. They cause social distress and leave chaos in their wake wherever they go. They often manipulate their way into leadership positions and can decimate organisations or even countries.

They have been linked, collectively, to deficits in empathy and increased aggression, however, the specific links are being examined in many different research programs. It is not clear if the lack of empathy is the dark core that drives indirect aggression, or if it is specific empathic trait deficits that are slightly different in each.

One recent study showed Narcissism to be differentiated from the other two in that there were higher levels of cognitive empathy, whereas they showed a greater lack of cognitive empathy of the affect (39).

Dark triad personalities are truly malignant 'energy vampires' and will deliberately target their victims without remorse. Although they are distinct traits there is a lot of overlap, and all three are associated with a callous-manipulative interpersonal style (40). They are considered the three personality variables that contribute the most to aversive social behaviour.

They score low on Agreeableness and Conscientiousness in the Big 5, but some show Neuroticism. Some dark triad personalities, however, do show Altruism, but only when it is perceived that the altruism would benefit them personally (41).

Narcissism

This trait is characterised by:

- egotism
- pride
- grandiosity
- dominance
- lack of affective empathy
- unwilling or unable to identify with other's feelings
- high on Extraversion and Openness

Malignant narcissism, a particularly severe form,

presents with:

- grandiose narcissism
- paranoia
- sadism
- anti-social behaviours
- lack of moral reasoning
- aggression

Machiavellianism

Characterised by:

- focus on self-interest
- deception
- manipulation of others
- exploitation
- lack of morality (cynical disregard for)
- unprincipled
- cold
- suspicious
- low on Agreeableness and Conscientiousness

Psychopathy

The most malevolent of the dark triad personalities, and characterised by severe:

- selfishness
- impulsivity
- thrill-seeking
- antisocial behaviour
- callousness
- lack of remorse
- lack of cognitive empathy for affect
- not distress by the suffering of victims
- low on Agreeableness, Conscientiousness and Neuroticism (secondary psychopathy can score high on Neuroticism)

Main characteristics of the Dark Triad personality traits Source: D'Souza (2016). (42)

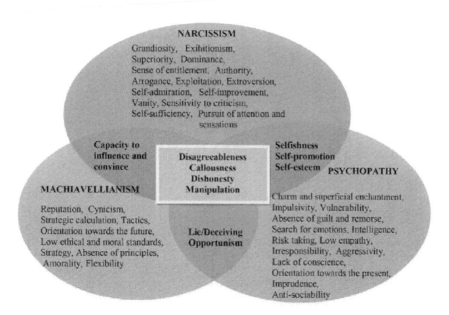

NARCISSISM

Grandiosity, Exihitionism, Superiority, Dominance, Sense of entitlement, Authority, Arrogance, Exploitation, Extroversion, Self-admiration, Self-improvement, Vanity, Sensitivity to criticism, Self-sufficiency, Pursuit of attention and sensations

Capacity to influence and convince

MACHIAVELLIANISM

Reputation, Cynicism, Strategic calculation, Tactics, Orientation towards the future, Low ethical and moral standards, Strategy, Absence of principles, Amorality, Flexibility

Disagreeableness Callousness Dishonesty Manipulation

Lie/Deceiving Opportunism

Selfishness Self-promotion Self-esteem PSYCHOPATHY

Charm and superficial enchantment, Impulsivity, Vulnerability, Absence of guilt and remorse, Search for emotions, Intelligence, Risk taking, Low empathy, Irresponsibility, Aggressivity, Lack of conscience, Orientation towards the present, Imprudence, Anti-sociability

Why do they target empaths?

Manipulative personalities such as the dark triad personalities will see a source of energy – a 'free ride' so to speak, in empaths and HSP's.

They see a:

- loving, caring person
- full of warmth, giving generously
- will take care of them

- be devoted to them
- listen to what they say
- do what they are asked to do

They will also target anyone that appears to be:

- lonely, hurt
- low on self-esteem
- in need of a savior

They will present a false self, quite deliberately:

- charming
- intelligent
- giving
- caring
- interested in everything you are interested in
- invent a reason for you to take care of them emotionally (i.e. family rejection, divorce, lost child, the list of fake hurts is endless)

They will pick a target:

- very deliberately
- find out as much as they can about them before introducing themselves (even to the point of stalking) if possible
- fake openness and trustworthiness
- encourage you to share your deep secrets (and this is very seductive to the empath whom always get dumped with other's emotions and secrets)
- pledge to take care of you and protect you
- pathologically lie to impress you
- hint at their deep pain and need for healing to reel you in

Once the empath has taken the bait and is now connected to the manipulator, they will

- engage in confusing behavior
- getting angry about minor things
- then claiming it was just stress
- or you misunderstood

- or they did not get angry (gas lighting) it is your imagination
- promise never to do it again
- blame it on an abusive childhood

This behaviour gradually escalates over time, but the moment you do not do things in their way, they will:

- be cold
- punishing
- withholding
- emotionally abusive
- verbally abusive with jibes, dismissed as jokes
- recruiting your friends and family against you (triangulation)
- breaking down your sense of self
- making you mistrust your own judgment.

Often it becomes an abusive relationship in the extreme

- isolation – making sure you do not socialize or see your family or friends
- financially – withholding financial support and even controlling your money and resources
- sexually – demanding sexual intimacy whenever their needs dictate, irrespective of your feelings
- psychologically – breaking down your sense of self, gaslighting, triangulating
- emotionally – calling you hypersensitive and paranoid, sometimes even delusional
- physically – intimidation with threats of leaving, threats of violence or killing you or your family, and actual physical violence.

Empaths and Narcissists can create the 'Perfect Storm' of destructive relationships – the empath wants to heal the narcissist, whom callously just want to suck them dry emotionally, use up all their resources for his own benefit and leave them in chaos and destruction.

Hsps (Highly Sensitive Persons)

About 15 to 20% of people have a psychological trait that is known as Sensory Processing Sensitivity (SPS) (35). This is not the same as the disorder known as Sensory Processing Disorder, but there are similar signs and symptoms.

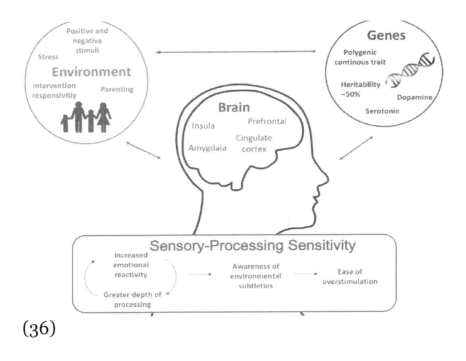

(36)

Highly Sensitive Persons (HSP) (34) has been

recognized as a personality trait.

HSP's show signs of extreme sensitivity to emotions, crowds, light, sound, and touch. Recent research has concentrated on the theory of differential susceptibility to the environment. (35) They do not, however, absorb the emotions and energy from other people, the way empaths do.

They are often called shy or timid, even introverted, but a large portion of HSP's are actually extroverted. They are unusually creative and often intellectually gifted.

Medics, Medications And Misdiagnoses

Extreme mood swings and unaccounted for sadness and depression may lead an empath, whom has not yet learned the reasons for them picking up so many diverse emotions in a short time, and whom does not have a clear self-them understanding, to think there is something wrong.

Overworked and inattentive medical staff may misdiagnose an empath as having social anxiety, bipolar disorder illness or borderline personality disorder.

There are however differences that we need to understand.

Social Anxiety

Many people experience mild forms of social anxiety when in a new social situation or having to present a talk or paper in a public forum, and introverts or shy people may just simply not enjoy big crowds or new people.

With social anxiety though, these normal social situations make them so uncomfortable and cause such extreme stress that they avoid it at all cost.

Social anxiety or phobia is a mental condition, presenting as 'an intense and very persistent fear of being watched or judged by others' (36). It interferes with everyday activities such as school, work and other social situations, making it very hard to keep friends. They are intensely afraid of humiliation, being judged or rejected.

In social situations they will display symptoms of anxiety, such as sweating, rapid heartbeat, nausea, rigid body posture, averting eyes, speaking very softly, and often blanking out. They will avoid social contact as much as possible.

Differences between social anxiety and the empath:

- People with social anxiety are not naturally drawn to others, children or animals.
- People are not comfortable talking to them nor spilling their secrets and anxieties to them

- They do not easily make friends like an empath does.
- Their avoidance of crowds or groups of people is constant and ongoing and grounded in fear of humiliation and rejection.
- This is quite unlike the empath that needs to recharge in quiet and may from time to time avoid others to protect themselves from overload.

Bipolar

As empaths may experience wild emotional swings during a day, due to them absorbing the emotions and energy surrounding them, they may appear to be mentally and emotionally unstable to the uninformed. If they are not aware of the implications of their empathic traits, they may seek medical input and may be misdiagnosed as being bipolar.

Bipolar Disorder is a mental health condition, also known as manic depression that causes unusual and extreme mood swings. Mania or hypomania presents as euphoric feelings, feeling very energetic or incredibly irritable. In the depression phase, the person feels sad, low, blue, hopeless and loses interest in most pleasurable activities. Episodes may occur rarely or often and can last anything from days to weeks to months (36).

It affects sleep, activity and judgment and often leads to irrational and illogical thought patterns and behavior, and reality distortions.

The extreme highs and lows differ from person to person, and the disease affects everyone differently. Both bipolar disorder and empaths display extreme emotions, however, there are huge differences in the source and type and duration of emotions. Cognitive empathy is low in Bipolar disorder (45).

Main Differences

- A Bipolar sufferer can become reckless or out of control during a manic episode.
- Empaths are much more in control of their emotions and will withdraw if they become overwhelmed.
- During bipolar manic episodes, the episodes last much longer, even days, whereas the mood swings of the empath are much shorter and related to the energy they absorb from the people and the environment surrounding them at the time.
- Bipolar disorder sufferers are much less likely to display empathy towards others, whereas empaths have very high levels of empathy.

Bpd

Borderline Personality Disorder is a mental disorder characterised by the person displaying 'an ongoing pattern of varying moods, self-image, and behaviour.' (37)

It is characterized by extensive behavioural and interpersonal problems related to cognitive and emotional dysfunction, and they have low cognitive empathy (46). This manifests as mood swings, intense episodes of depression, anxiety and anger that can last from a few hours to days. They are uncertain of self and their role in the world so can change values, interests and opinions at breakneck speed.

They see the world in black and white and can switch on friends and loved ones in a heartbeat, swinging from idealisation to devaluation, which leads to incredibly intense and unstable relationships.

They suffer chronic feelings of emptiness, a distorted self-image, dissociation and often partake in dangerous and reckless behaviours such as binge eating, alcohol or drug abuse, unsafe sex, spending sprees, and reckless driving. They demonstrate highly impulsive behaviours. They also show an abnormal fear of abandonment.

Differences Between Bpd And The Empath

- Empaths never experience feelings of emptiness
- They do not fear abandonment, but rather the opposite of being swallowed up in a relationship when their self-other distinction is not well developed.
- They may share mood swings, but the nature of the mood swings is different, an empath's sadness lasts as long as the person they picked up the sadness from.
- They may both resort to unsafe behaviours, however, the BPD does it to fill an ever-present gaping hole and the empath tries to numb themselves from an overload of input.
- Empaths remain loyal and caring and always has a big heart.

Of course, an empath may have an underlying mental

problem, but those cases are far and few between.

Protecting Yourself

Learn How To Protect Yourself As An Empath

Whilst the wonderful positive gifts of the empath can greatly enrich the individual's life, it is important to learn how to use these gifts appropriately so as to protect yourself.

The dark side of being an empath can be a real threat to your physical, mental, emotional and social health, and it is a slippery slope to emotional burnout, or worse, being trapped in abusive relationships, if you do not establish a firm sense of self, boundaries and accommodations for your sensitivities and emotions.

If you find yourself with symptoms of:

- Fuzzy thinking
- short temper
- droopy eyelids
- feelings of guilt
- emotional exhaustion,

- fueling with caffeine, or
- drinking more alcohol than usual

It is definitely time to sit back and reassess and find a way back to yourself.

But how do you protect yourself against this in the first place?

How do you lead a rich and fulfilling life without constantly having to be on your guard?

What steps can you put in place to ensure you don't fall victim to emotional and sensory overload?

Strategies For Handling The Challenges Of Feeling And Absorbing So Many Stimuli

Broad strategies and common advice dished out to empaths on how to handle the challenges of feeling so much, or absorbing so many stimuli, typically include one or more of the following:

- Learn how to embrace your gift of feeling so deeply or how to recognize your own emotions.
- Manage stress
- Exercise regularly, sleep well
- Confide in your friends
- Talk to a therapist
- Remember the temporary nature of feeling overwhelmed, i.e. this too shall pass
- Tell people in your work or social circles that you become overwhelmed in noisy environments
- Explain that retreating to a quiet place will help
- Practice self-compassion, refrain from criticizing yourself.

The Four R's

Building a strategy to protect yourself for the long haul requires a comprehensive plan, with clear to-dos and long-term goals.

A good place to start this strategy is to draw a map, outline the overall goals, and the broad steps to take to achieve them, as well as practical hands-on advice on how to implement the plan.

The three R's model (recognize – reverse – resilience) is often used as a starting point by psychologists, however, it may be prudent to take a step back, to start at the beginning with setting clear goals, namely reevaluating your priorities. What is it that you would like to see in the long term? Where do you want to be? How do you want to feel and act?

Thus, the Four R's (53):

- Reevaluate
- Recognize
- Resilience
- Reverse

Let us look at each in turn.

Reevaluate Priorities

Decide if you want to live your life proactively, leading to a rich and fulfilling existence, or if you are satisfied to be dragged from episode to episode of emotional exhaustion and eventually burnout, trying to survive and maybe hiding out as much as possible to avoid any further overload.

- Commit to loving yourself enough to engage actively in self-care.
- Commit to understanding your gifts and the potential problems so as to build a strong resistance.
- Commit to building resilience so as to bounce back no matter what life throws at you.

Whilst most people will claim that their priorities are very important to them, very few could list them, nor rank them. Even less will make the time to ensure that they are aligning their daily actions to their priorities.

The late Steven Covey, in his pioneering book 'The 7 Habits of Highly Effective People', presented the world with a simple framework for evolving into a highly effective person. Whilst it was snapped up by the business community as a 'how to manage your time better' guideline, its truly enduring messages are that

- change starts from within,
- you must begin with the end in mind, and the most profound
- Put First Things First.

This is what reevaluating your priorities and giving depth and meaning to your life, are all about.

Remember the story of the teacher that gave her class items to put in a glass jar? They started with a layer of sand, then a layer of gravel, then small stones, and finally big stones. However by this time, the jar was full, and there was no space for the bigger stones.

She then taught the class to see

- the stones as the most important things in our lives, for example, our health, our family, things we cannot live without. And to always put first things first.
- The small stones represent the things that matter to you a great deal, but that you can live without – so if you only had big stones, your life would still be full, as they are not essential to your wellbeing.
- The gravel represents the 'nice-to-have' things in your life, a well-deserved vacation, a spa treatment, a special set of books. Things that make life fun and exciting, but not essential in the real sense of the word.
- The sand represents the fillers, the things that you do because you feel obliged to but that does not bring you any joy, or the useless things we

buy because it is on sale or someone else has one and loves it.

If you put the big stones in first, then the smaller ones, then the gravel, and lastly the least important, the sand, there is often room for it all – but that is not really the point, you need to clarify what are the things to put first.

If you constantly fill your glass with sand and gravel, you will never have space for the most important things in your life.

This 'rock, pebble and sand' analogy is also often used as a time management training tool. However, we are not talking about time management per se, we are talking about your emotional and mental wellbeing, which is much more important.

But, where do you start?

Steps To Take Action

Write them down

If you have never done this before, it may take a few days or even weeks to get them into a format that will be easy to remember or that makes sense to you.

Start by jotting down a few notes – anywhere that works for you, on a notepad, or in your Notes on your smartphone, or a journal. Go back to your list every day and add to it, or make changes, or clarify what you meant.

It needs to make sense to you, you do not have to put down lofty ideals that you think someone else wants to see, or that will make you look good. Be honest, what really matters to you. You can play a game with yourself, for instance, if you had to pick three to five things that you cannot or do not want to give up, ever, what would it be? Play this with your friends, it may help you clarify your priorities.

Rank Your Priorities

Once you have a consolidated list, rank them in order of importance. It will help you clarify your needs and be a constant reminder to spend your time and energy where it matters most.

Turn Them Into Actions

A list of priorities is not of much use unless you can translate them to your daily life. Turn them into something you can do – for each priority list a number of action steps.

For example, if 'family' was one of your priorities, some action steps may be 'gadget-free family meals' or 'read a story to my child every night'.

Review

The old adage 'you cannot manage what you cannot measure' applies here too. It does not mean measuring activity as you would at work, but you do need to monitor yourself, and see where you are sticking to your commitments and priorities and what is slipping. And slipping is almost guaranteed, life happens, no matter the most carefully laid plans.

Regular reviewing and monitoring of your priorities will help you keep on track, remind you of what is really important in life, and help you not 'sweat the small stuff'.

For the empath, this means having to really focus on yourself, your loved ones and your long-term goals, and not being sidetracked and hooked by your need to help others, which often leads to the exclusion of your family and your own emotional health.

Maybe posting them on your bathroom mirror, or

your fridge, or the side of your computer screen, or even turning a shot of them into the wallpaper on your smartphone, will ensure that you see them on a regular basis, and help you keep on track.

Action Expresses Priorities.

If you neglect your priorities, your life is likely to become unstable. Clarifying your priorities is about building a strong foundation for yourself like you would if you built a house.

Building a strong foundation includes making self-care a priority for the empath. But how do you build self-care into your life?

Self-Care

Self-care is not a luxury we get to indulge in every now and then. It is about your respecting yourself enough to care for your overall health.

Living a healthier, fulfilling life is about creating balance in all spheres of health.

Everything Is Connected

Compartmentalization may work as a strategy for very short periods of time but can be very damaging. Your mental, emotional, social, spiritual, financial, and physical health are all interconnected, and as is your environment and lifestyle choices

Eliminate Stress

A reasonable amount of stress can motivate you to do what needs to be done, however persistent, long-term stress can wreak havoc with your life and health. Either make serious efforts to change the situation or remove yourself from the situation.

Live In The Moment

Longing for the 'good old days' or thinking if only I had 'x' will definitely make you miserable and have you losing out on life. Enjoy every moment. You can control how you react to what is happening right now.

Appreciate What You Have

Focus on the positives in your life and stop trying to compete with the Joneses.

Take A Long-Term View On Health

This means getting vaccinated as required, avoiding polluted areas, doing your required check-ups when necessary and being cognizant of any genetic-based risks in health and what steps you need to take to protect yourself.

Live A Healthful Life

Chasing every latest fad on the internet is one of the

worst things you can possibly do. Follow the science, read up on healthy living at verified scientific sites, for example, Mayo Clinic, Harvard, AHA, etc.

Get Moving!

It does not really matter how, do whatever you enjoy and that does not cause pain or discomfort. Moving at least once an hour during the day brings untold health benefits.

Exercise

- reduces stress,
- increases energy and
- produces feel-good hormones.

Make Every Meal A Feast!

Feasting is not just for special occasions, a treat, or a guilty pleasure. Prepare healthy balanced meals as a feast to look forward to and enjoy every sensuous bite. Include proteins, lots of fruit, vegetables, and healthy grains. Enjoy your glass of wine or cup of coffee.

Avoid Any Form Of Substance Abuse

Find a way to quit smoking, and if you have any other substance abuse problems, get help.

Hydrate

Drinking enough water or eating fruits and food with high water content such as orange or cucumber slices helps

- keep you hydrated throughout the day,
- minimizes the load on the heart,
- assists muscle and joint movement,
- removes waste and
- maintains your temperature.

Sleep

Getting enough quality sleep is important for

- healing damaged cells,
- boosting your immune system,
- stabilizing weight hormones,
- recharging the cardiovascular system.
- helps with learning through a process called memory consolidation.

Sleep deprivation leads to:

- irritability,
- moodiness and a
- greater risk for accidents.

Take Breaks

Self-care includes taking regular breaks to revitalize. It includes small and longer breaks, and the benefits include

- increased productivity and creativity,

- memory consolidation and improved learning,
- restore motivation and
- decrease decision fatigue.

Prioritize Your Close Relationships

Investing in what is most important in the long term, by giving your full attention to your closest relationship, will bring feelings of self-worth, satisfaction and warmth. Enjoy, have fun and be all there.

Socialize

Quit being so serious and have some fun with your social groups. Regular social contact and connecting are more important to health than diet and exercise.

Believe In Something

Spirituality and religious belief are beneficial to longevity. It may be something as simple as believing in kindness or paying-it-forward. Finding meaning in any form can benefit your health and others.

Show Gratitude

Practicing gratitude helps you focus on the positive, and leads to

- increased levels of well-being,
- self-control,
- optimism and
- happiness.
- It helps strengthen interpersonal relationships.

Recognise

Learn To Recognise Your Own Feelings

Once you become more self-aware you will be able to pick up on your own feelings and recognise symptoms of discomfort or overload.

Distinguish Between Emotions You Carry On Behalf Of Another Person And Your Own Emotions

This may be a little bit harder, when you absorb so much emotional distress and energy from others the line between what you are feeling and what they were feeling can become a little bit blurred.

Think about how you felt before you started engaging with this particular person,

- What was your mood like? What did they talk about during the interaction?
- What was their mood like during the interaction?
- Did they feel better, calmer, more centered after the interaction?
- Did you pick up their bad mood, or emotional distress, frustration or anger during the conversation or visit?
- Is this the first time this happened with this person or do you frequently pick up their emotional distress to your own detriment?

Don t Fight Negative Feelings

Don't try to make yourself feel better by masking negative feelings.

If you have picked up another individual's distress and negative energy, admit that it is not yours, and distance yourself from it.

If you are feeling sad or hurt, frustrated or angry, identify the emotion, the cause of it, and determine if it is something you can fix or not.

If not accept the feeling as part of your growth, and work through it.

Stay In The Present

Understand that all feelings have a transient nature, and that recognising the feeling, and choosing to move forward will help you to eventually lift your mood

Do not engage in morbid rumination about the interaction, or previous acts or omissions, and how things could be different 'if only' you did something differently.

Do not engage in wishful thinking about how you will retaliate or do better in future or how things could be different 'if only' you had something else.

Stay in the present, feel your feelings but give yourself a time-limit before moving on.

Resilience

Empaths are often told 'you are hypersensitive' or 'you need to develop a thicker skin', which can be very unfair and hurtful.

One of the most critical strategies for protecting yourself is to build resilience.

What Is Resilience?

Resilience is the ability to recover quickly from difficulties, to bounce back so to speak. It hints at toughness, like the ability of an object to spring back into shape.

Some people cave under adversity, responding with a flood of emotions and a very strong sense of uncertainty and confusion. Those with strong resilience, that cultivate their skills are able to not only mitigate the effects of adverse events but can adapt to them and return to normal functioning or even better, thriving, relatively quickly.

Resilience is 'that ineffable quality that allows some people to be knocked down by life and come back at least as strong as before' (53)

It does not mean that they do not experience pain and sadness or distress, the road to resilience is paved with considerable emotion and distress. However, it involves thoughts, actions and behaviors that can be learnt.

Resilience Factors

According to the American Psychological Association (APA), factors that contribute to resilience include:

- Caring and supportive relationships (family and other) that
- Create trust and love
- Provide role models
- Offer encouragement
- Reassurance
- A Positive view of self
- Confidence in your strengths and abilities
- Capacity to make realistic plans
- Take steps to carry out those plans

- Capacity to manage your impulses
- Manage strong feelings

When you have resilience, you can access or harness that inner strength to help you cope when adversity strikes.

When you lack resilience, you may feel victimized, ruminate, become overwhelmed or turn to unhealthy coping mechanisms such as overeating or substance abuse.

Resilience gives you the ability to see past current problems, deal with stress and find fulfillment and enjoyment. It protects against mental problems and improves your ability to cope.

The psychological resources required to cushion the deleterious effects of stress or suffering makes up the essence of Resilience:

- Strong self-esteem,
- Optimism,
- Mastery of your emotions,
- Ability to see failure as feedback

Optimism can blunt the impact of the adverse events on the mind and body. This allows access to cognitive resources to evaluate what happened and how different behavioural paths could have generated more productive outcomes, in a cool and objective manner.

How To Build Resilience For The Empath

Know yourself and limits

Be clear on your goals and what you can or cannot handle. This means that you do not have to push past your own limits if it affects your mental and emotional health.

Advice can be confusing, yes you need to stretch

yourself, but in a positive way, doing new things that excite you and enriches your life.

Accepting behaviour and inputs from others that pushes way past your limits of emotional inputs will damage your inner peace, disorient and confuse you and leave you emotionally drained.

Learn to recognise when you have had enough, and walk away, maybe for a few minutes to regroup, or for good. Be firm and consistent with your limits and draw a line in the sand.

If you tell a loved one or friend that they are crossing a line, expect them to respect that line, every time. If you draw a line one day, and the next time they cross it, you allow that to happen, maybe because you are too exhausted to point it out, or you just cannot be bothered as nothing changes, nothing will change. They will continue to cross your lines because you allow it.

Strengthen your sense of me-them

Do not get lost in blurred lines between your feelings and that of others.

Theory of Mind is a very important social-cognitive skill that develops over time in young children, where we learn to think about your own and other's mental states, and helps you understand that other people may think differently to yourself.

So in essence, what we think is going on in someone else's mind is just our theory. For the empath, whom feel other's emotions and absorb them like a sponge would water, it is important to strengthen the theory of mind, to understand, at a cognitive level, that you may sense the other person's feelings, but you do not fully comprehend what they are thinking.

Thus, if you sense sadness, it does not mean that they

would experience sadness the way you would, or be sad for the same reasons. You need to identify, if for instance you suddenly feel sad in another's presence, whose feeling it really is, yours or theirs? This takes practice in real life and can be hard to overcome, but it is a strong building block in strengthening your sense of self and building your resilience.

Notice your suffering

Be ruthless with naming your suffering for what it is, giving too much, feeling too much, this way you can learn to say no when you need to.

Empaths often suffer in silence, in order to help others, and can do immeasurable harm to their own mental health by not acknowledging nor naming their suffering.

Putting it out there, verbally, makes it real, takes it out the closet, and opens the path for you to learn to set boundaries and say no to protect yourself.

Practice self-compassion

Give yourself a break and accept that change is part of life and a mistake is just another opportunity to learn.

Be kind to yourself at all times. Allow yourself the compassion you so generously dole out to others.

You can have an empathic conversation with yourself in the mirror – it will help you see how hard you are on yourself.

Learn to control your emotions

Which might be really hard to do, especially for the emotional empath - you have to practice this all the time.

If you allow your emotions to get the better of you,

you hand over your power. Emotional reactions blur your ability to think logically and make proper decisions. You end up splashing and drowning in a pool of negativity and emotions.

If a child accidentally fell into a pool you would tell him to stay calm, tread water and stop thrashing, so you can talk him to the edge of the pool or get in to go get him. Controlling your emotions works in exactly the same way. Take a deep breath, don't lash out, tell yourself this is not the end of the world, regroup and find something to distract you until you can think more clearly.

Some people count to ten, others have found help by using the anxiety-busting coping mechanism to identify

- Five things you see around you
- Four things you can touch around you
- Three things you hear
- Two things you can smell

- One thing you can taste

Concentrate on maintaining calmness.

Control your reactions

To other's comments, actions or omissions and emotions. You cannot stop how you feel in the moment, but you can learn to control your reaction to that feeling, that is where your real power lies.

When you feel yourself wanting to jump in and fix things, or tell them what to do, or what you really think, or what the actual truth is, stop yourself.

Take a moment to breathe in and out a few times and try to clarify your feeling. Then make an attempt to be logical about what was said or what happened, and only respond when you are ready to do so calmly.

For the empath, the major obstacle to overcome in

controlling their reactions is to stop taking the bait hook line and sinker.

Do not jump in to come to the rescue all the time. Sit back and let the person talk and give him space to try figure it out for himself.

In most cases if he is not able to figure out a solution himself, it is because he does not want to solve the problem, he is simply manipulating you to do his bidding and disguising it as an emotional conundrum.

Accept that you cannot help every person you meet.

Keep Perspective

Stop seeing every setback as an insurmountable problem, learn to control how you interpret and respond to these events.

Learn to distinguish between an event, your life and yourself as a person of substance.

Take criticism grain of salt, and consider the source.

Make Connections

Build meaningful and deep relationships

- with family and friends,
- join social groups, faith-based or spiritual organizations or
- find volunteer opportunities.

Asking for and accepting support and connection (circling the wagons) is a big factor in building resilience.

Evaluate your close friends

Take a good look at your close friends and your intimate social circle.

Do they provide you with love, laughter, support, positivity, and uplifting experiences?

Do you look forward to seeing them or do you feel dread when they call to meet up?

Do they talk about interesting events or activities that you and others in your circle may be interested in, or do they only talk about themselves and their achievements or problems?

Are you able to have deep and meaningful conversations with them above life, or do they shy away from anything that is not superficial?

Do they respect others, their parents, their family, their colleagues, and friends and try to lift them up, or do they spend their time gossiping about others and breaking them down? Do they think denigrating others, especially their parents, make them cool?

Are you comfortable sharing deep feelings or secrets with them, or do you wonder if you can trust them with something so personal?

Are you comfortable asking them for support and understanding when you need it, or do you feel they may belittle you or attack you if you show any perceived weakness?

Do they accept you with all your idiosyncrasies or do they constantly tell you to do better or how to change yourself?

Do they respect your boundaries or do they expect you to do their bidding and get angry or withdraw if you do not comply with their requirements?

If there is nothing but negativity let them go or they

will drag you down

Ignore your inner critic

You need to stop criticizing yourself and give up on perfectionism – it is time to slay the dragons and live in the present.

Everyone has insecurities and fears, maybe a bad memory or two that nags at them day in and day out. It is the individual that can convince themselves that whatever went wrong is now firmly in the past and that every mistake or put down is an opportunity to learn.

strong self-esteem and sense of self will also help you see that whatever was or is said to you is just another's opinion and does not necessarily constitute the truth.

Einstein is famously quoted for saying ,'everyone is a

genius, but if you judge a fish by its ability to climb a tree, it will live its whole life believing that it is stupid'.

Whilst there is no evidence that he actually said this, it holds universal truths in that we all have different skills and abilities and we have our own innate genius – it is absurd to judge everyone according to one standard, especially yourself, but it also points to the issue of self-belief, it is equally absurd to spend your life believing you are stupid because someone else said you are.

Set Healthy Boundaries

Everything in life is interlinked and setting healthy boundaries is part of building self-esteem and resilience

- communicate how you feel openly and honestly,
- take responsibility for your own happiness,
- follow through on what you say,
- expect your boundaries to be respected,

- take responsibility for your own actions
- never assume or guess the other person's feelings
- know and accept when you need to move on.

Nurture a positive self-image

See yourself as

- strong and rational,
- able to solve problems,
- trust your instincts and
- do not allow yourself being preyed on

Set Realistic Goals

Clarify your goals, write them down and then purposefully pursue them.

Make sure they are your goals and not those of your loved ones or friends.

Small victories will strengthen your resolve and resilience.

Reclaim your power and pursue your own dreams.

It may be as simple as making time for half an hour of practicing a hobby you enjoy after you have put the kids to bed, or as grand and far-reaching as you can imagine.

Make your day Meaningful

Do things you enjoy and will give you a sense of purpose and meaning

At the end of each day, you need to be able to look at at least a few things that you really enjoyed, and that you are grateful for.

Make a habit of reviewing the day in a few minutes of quiet time before bed, put aside the things that went wrong to deal with later, and be grateful for what you enjoyed.

Be Proactive

Don't ignore problems by playing ostrich and hiding your head in the sand, if you suspect something may happen or go wrong.

Figure out what needs to be done to Prevent it, fix it, or mitigate the effects if it cannot be fixed.

Then make a plan of action and implement it.

Get professional help

If you feel that you are not making progress building resilience, or if you do not know where to start, approach a professional for assistance. It is imperative for your mental well-being, and time and money well spent.

- **Reflect their feelings back to them**

To ensure that you do not take on everyone else's emotional garbage, learn how to reflect their feelings back to them

- **Allow venting for specific amounts of time only**

If you have friends or colleagues or intimate partners that are always upset and living from one drama to the next, set limits to the amount of time they are allowed to vent per encounter. If they are frustrated or angry or upset with a specific situation, limit the length of time they can vent for (say six months for the loss of a partner) before they have to move on and

- **Learn to say 'Not my monkey'**

Every time you find yourself engaging in someone else's affairs or frustrations, remind yourself what is really important for you to deal with, and what the other person's own responsibilities are.

- **Commit to 'No more walking on eggshells'**

If someone makes you so uncomfortable that you feel like you have to tiptoe around them or 'walk on eggshells' it is time to set very strong boundaries or move on

- **Negotiate a compromise**

With that very obsessive-compulsive person in your life – whom wants everything done just so according to their requirements. Tell them what you can and cannot commit to and negotiate a compromise that will suit both of you.

- **Reclaim your power**

By pursuing your own goals, dreams and friendships rather than just follow those of other people in your life. Try out new things you have always wanted to do, go out and make new friends that will enhance your life

- **Detox from toxic people**

By taking time for yourself to recharge and restore your energy levels even if it is just a short break

- **Shielding**

In the moment is a good strategy if you start to feel overwhelmed, however, it is not a sustainable long-term coping mechanism. Shielding involves visualizing yourself building an imaginary shield around you to protect you from the onslaught of inputs (like a bubble that cannot be penetrated)

- **Spend some time in nature**

Go for a walk, or plan a hiking holiday, spend some time on the beach, walk barefoot on the lawn, do some gardening or play with your dog.

- **Practice Mindfulness**

This means becoming aware of the actual moment you are in. Mastering mindfulness takes practice and getting some assistance can help you to use it to ground yourself even during interactions to help you control your emotions.

Emotional Vampires And Dark Triad Traits

Malevolent and non-malevolent Emotional Vampires can wreak havoc with an Empath's emotions and sanity. Specific tactics to deal with emotional vampires include:

- **Get support** from your friends (circle the wagons) by opening up and explaining to them what you are dealing with and ask for help.

- **Get to know the enemy** and how they operate. Learn about the different types of emotional vampires and the tactics they employ to hook you.

- Identify and learn what **your particular hooks** are, and look out for them when meeting new people, or dealing with people currently in your life.

- **Know who you are dealing with**, do not underestimate the chaos and damage an emotional vampire can leave in their wake. Be brave and concede that you may have been fooled by a very experienced trickster.

- **Avoid making hasty decisions** about anything related to the emotional vampire, and do not cave to pressure if you are uncomfortable with any interaction with them

- Emotional vampires can be very **predictable**, making your escape easier

- **Get the upper hand** by observing them from multiple angles, enlist the help of friends to help clarify their tactics and manipulations

- **Learn to walk away** from emotional vampires for good, sometimes going NO contact is the only way forward and cutting the cord becomes essential for your emotional freedom

- **Don't try to reason** with an emotional vampire, it is a complete waste of time, as they are not interested in reason but only their own agenda, rather use your mental resources for selfcare

- Emotional vampires are **deeply unhappy** people, they are insecure and weak and will show no goodwill, so do not make excuses for them or try and cover for them

- **Avoid their emotions** at all cost, lest it infects your mood, if you cannot separate yourself from the person (i.e. your boss or family member)

- **If they show rage**, keep your distance as far as possible, show a poker face, be very stoic, and show them that their emotions do not affect yours.

- **If they start an argument**, do not get others dragged in and avoid taking sides at all costs.

- **Do not fall prey to their manipulations**, be on the lookout for them and stick to your resolve to deal with them in a mature and calm manner.

- **You can show compassion** but set limits on the emotional diplomacy you display; this will free you from their hold over you and reduce the emotional drain

- **Clarify your relationships** with anyone showing emotional vampire traits, and walk away if your circumstances allow; if it affects you too severely walk away anyway and deal with the consequences as they may arise.

- **Focus intently** when you deal with an emotional vampire, remind yourself constantly that your aim is not rehabilitation, some people cannot be 'saved', but counter them with common grace

Specific tips for dealing with the:

Narcissist

- Set realistic expectations, and remind yourself they won't change
- Ensure that your self-worth is not dependent on the other person
- Do not confide your deepest feelings or divulge any secrets as they will use it against you
- If contact is unavoidable your best tactic is to engage in the tedious ego stroking, they crave without getting emotionally involved
- However, the best strategy is no contact

Victim

- Set kind but very firm limits
- Do not pander to their pity party
- Listen briefly then ask for solutions

- Use your body language to enforce limits you have set
- Do not offer to solve their problems, even if it is the quickest way to get them away from you
- If they behave in a paranoid way, empathize with their emotions but do not engage in facts
- Show them clearly that you are not condoning their behavior
- Keep your distance

Controller

- Be assertive and calm
- Never try to control a controller, it will not end well
- Don't tell them what to do and do not consult with them
- Explain that you appreciate their opinion, but that you need to do this yourself
- If an intervention is required, change the subject, or try to get them into a group of people to diffuse the moment

Constant talker

- They do not respond to nonverbal clues so you will have to speak up and interrupt them, no matter how tough it may be for you to do so
- If you need an escape, claim a prior appointment and leave or show them the door.
- Do not indulge them in any way

Drama queen

- Remember they can't draw energy from equanimity, so stay calm and take deep breaths
- Count silently in your head to restore or maintain your mental equilibrium
- Know your priorities and concentrate on that
- Do not get yourself caught up in their histrionics or try to offer advice or help
- Set limits and stick to them

Reverse - How To Recharge When You Get Over-Cooked '

Remember that

- a strong self-esteem,
- optimism,
- mastery of your emotions and
- the ability to learn from mistakes

constitute the psychological resources to buffer you from the deleterious effects of stress and emotional overload.

Whilst making self-care the foundation of your long-term health, and requires discipline and commitment, life sometimes gets in the way and tosses a few curved balls at you.

If you are feeling emotionally frazzled or 'over-cooked' you need to make a concerted effort to reverse the effects of this overload.

Some ideas that work particularly well for the empath includes:

Slow Down

Deliberately force yourself to slow down. If this means withdrawing completely, then that is what you need to do. You may simply space out social commitments a bit further apart, or schedule in some time for yourself in a busy day, or make sure that you fit in activities that will quieten your frantic mind.

Reflect

Take time to reflect on what brought you here to this point. You may feel like a long-distance runner that is out of breath with legs starting to cramp, but you need to stop, take deep breaths, and then reflect on the events leading up to this point. No recriminations, no guilt-tripping, simply look at it as objectively as possible and then tell yourself it is OK to take a break to recharge.

Learn from each event, so as to help yourself to prepare in the future to avoid the overload. Understand though that you cannot have fool-proof plans, somethings hit you harder than others, and you just need to learn to ride it out.

Heal

Allow yourself the time to heal properly before resurfacing, in whichever way works for you. You may need to scrub your kitchen or alphabetize your books, or lie on the beach for a whole day doing nothing but listen to the waves, or jump out of a plane with a parachute to feel the peace of free-floating, the number of ways to heal is as many as there are empaths.

Rediscover Nature

Most empaths find soothing and healing in nature. They need to be able to commune with the outdoors, the peace and quiet of being away from the hustle and bustle of cities and offices and busy lives.

A walk in a park, a nice long hike up in the mountains where the air is fresh, the river water cool, brownish and refreshing and the soil damp from decomposing leaves.

Or the sting of the sun and the hot wind on your cheeks out in the desert, with nothing but miles and miles of sand and xerophytes to show us how to thrive in even the harshest conditions.

Maybe thundering down the white rapids at breakneck speed or flying from tree to tree on a zip line in a rain forest. Catching a big wave on your surfboard or flying down a ski slope on your board.

Many will choose something sedate though, pottering in your garden, picking herbs for your dinner, doing quiet but long laps in a tranquil ocean or pool, playing catch with your dog in the park, or watching the sun set whilst having a picnic.

Express Your Needs

It is vitally important that you express your needs to your intimate partners and close family and friends. Explain how an overload of sensory inputs affects your mental and emotional state, what you need to do to cope and how to ground yourself.

It is important to communicate that it is about your reaction to sensory overload and that you are asking for basic accommodation and understanding. This will prevent misunderstandings and unnecessary hurt feelings.

However, it is not acceptable to expect everyone to run their lives around your emotional and sensory issues, it must be a mutually respectful accommodation, a little bit of give and take on both sides. Use your gifts to make life better for all, not to manipulate others.

Resolve Conflicts

Whilst it may sound counterintuitive, as many of our frazzled states are caused by interpersonal conflicts, in our lives, or other's, the goal should always be to resolve conflicts.

Being there for someone is more productive than being right, and sometimes conflict sprouts from silly disagreements. Agree to disagree and move on.

If someone has insulted or hurt you, the best revenge is to forgive. Forgiving someone is not for their benefit, it is for yours, as it helps you to let go.

Let go of the hurt, the anger, the pain and the residual negative emotions that overload you. It frees you from emotional obligations and wasted time and energy.

Motivate Yourself To Take Steps Against Stress

When emotional exhaustion takes over or you are in full-blown emotional burnout, motivation levels are at an extreme low, and just reading a chapter on what to do can seem like too much to ask, never mind implementing any of these strategies, and that is all right too.

So, again, slow down, sometimes you must simply stop pushing the bicycle, rebalance, and then get on it to actually cycle.

Every thousand-mile journey starts with one step, according to ancient Chinese wisdom, and as trite as it may sound from time to time, it is a universal truth.

Take one step at a time, do what you can do, small victories will help build motivation to implement more. But do whatever you can to mitigate stress, as it affects your overall health and changes your body over the long term.

Break From Technology

A large part of our busyness is related to technology, and this constant connectedness can take a heavy toll on an empath, that needs periods of connecting and periods of withdrawal.

Take a break from technology, in whichever way you need to. Close the computer for a full weekend, do not check your email after work, set your smartphone to only allow through calls from loved ones during certain hours (this can be a lifesaver during overload) and commit to technology-free family meals.

Getting lost in a Netflix binge-watching session may help you unwind to start off with, but using it constantly is not a productive coping mechanism.

Minimise Sugar And Refined Carbs

When in overload, take a break from eating or drinking anything with high sugar content or refined carbs. You may think that your energy drink is keeping you going, it is, in fact, exacerbating your overload.

Hydrate with water, with maybe some fresh lemon slices, eat lots of fruit and don't be tempted to binge on large tubs of ice cream.

Omega-3

Making healthy food choices becomes compromised during overload or stressful situations. Remember to add Omega-3 Fatty Acid rich foods to your diet, it helps reduce anxiety and long-term inflammation (54).

Examples include

- Cold water fatty fish such as salmon, herring, tuna, mackerel and sardines
- Nuts and Seeds, for instance, almonds, walnuts, pistachios, chia or flaxseeds
- Plant oils, such as flaxseed oil or soybean oil.
- Fortified foods – eggs, juice, milk and milk products are often fortified with omega-3's

Minimize caffeine, trans fats and preservatives

Make sure that you minimize foods containing trans fats and preservatives, and if caffeine makes you jittery avoid it for a while.

Some empaths may need caffeine to calm down (rare but true) but must guard against taking their caffeine in sugared drinks. Plain brewed is best.

Meditate

Meditation is a learnt process, where you train your brain to focus and to practice redirecting your thoughts. Meditation teaches us to be present in the moment.

Meditation has many benefits, including

- Increased awareness of self and surrounding
- Reduces stress
- Helps control anxiety
- Develop concentration
- Improved mood
- Self-discipline
- Increased pain-tolerance
- Improved sleep patterns
- Generate kindness

Yoga

Yoga is an ancient practice that helps us bring together body and mind by incorporating poses, breathing techniques and meditation, to reduce stress and help with relaxation.

Benefits are immediate and long-term and may include

- Increase strength, flexibility and balance
- Reduce stress, anxiety and depression
- Improve sleep and relaxation
- Improve breathing
- Fight inflammation and improve quality of life.

Incorporating yoga practice in your daily routine can help you ground yourself, feel calmer and ready to deal with whatever you are facing.

Exercise

You need to exercise at least thirty minutes a day to

stay healthy, however, this can be hard to accomplish during overload. Motivate yourself to get dressed, for exercise, then to get off the couch, out the door and before you know it you are moving and feeling better.

Some will need to engage in extreme exercise to unwind, like a long run, or a hard game of racket-ball, or hitting a punch-bag. Others will prefer swimming, gardening or going for a walk in the park.

Do whatever helps you to get rid of all that negative energy and emotions.

Healing Water

For the empath being close to or in water can be very healing. Feeling the shower spray on your back or scalp, diving into the cool depths of a crystal-clear pool, soaking in a jet tub, or braving the waves in the ocean will help relax you and soothe your soul.

The feeling of being enveloped by water, the soothing sounds, the sense of weightlessness when in the water can all contribute to helping the empath relax and releasing negative energy.

Wind In Your Hair

Sometimes the empath just needs to feel the wind in their hair, to clear the muddle of emotions and energy in their minds.

Drive with the hood down, go on motorcycle rides, horseback riding, skydiving or go walk outside in windy conditions, and feel the cobwebs blow away

Volunteer

The last thing you need when in overload is more work and more caring, but paradoxically, volunteering can help you take your mind off your own problems, and even if just for the hour it takes to serve a meal to the homeless or walk a dog at the local

SPCA. It is an excellent way to restore perspective.

Vacation

It is tempting to take a vacation when in overload, the fantasy of getting away from it all, seeing new places, experiencing new cultures and cuisines may be just the break you need.

Do consider though your propensity to sensory overload when picking a vacation spot – a quiet retreat on a small island, or game reserve, or spa may be ideal, however, a jam-packed itinerary to a tourist destination may end up being the last nail in the coffin.

Boundaries

Revisit your boundaries, make sure they make sense and examine them for breaches. Communicate them kindly but clearly to those around you to avoid future problems

Shielding

Shielding (building an imaginary bubble around yourself) may be a useful technique in the short term to cope with sensory overload and having to deal with emotional vampires, as it mentally protects you and strengthens your defense against abuse.

It is however not an appropriate long-term strategy. You may need to learn to walk away. Distance and permanent solutions are great tools for enforcing emotional freedom.

Avoid Unavailable People And Dark Triad Relationships

In order to reverse the damage and give yourself time to heal, you must avoid the unavailable people that feel so comfortable to be around, and definitely not spend time around dark triad personalities. Being around them during healing periods would be equivalent to trying to swim in the desert sands.

If You Are Struggling, Get Professional Help

Knowing yourself and your limits are crucial to not only setting a course for yourself, but also for recovery.

If you are experiencing emotional burnout or are struggling to maintain boundaries and commit to healing, get professional help.

Your general practitioner or primary care provider can refer you to an appropriate mental health care professional, to assist you in this process.

There are many volunteer organizations that provide access to professional help in you are not in a financial position to do so on your own.

Be Present

Be present today, be open to yourself, and be open to the others around you. (13)☐Living in the moment, letting go of what was and what could be, is the most powerful way to heal yourself.

Stop beating yourself up for what you have or have not done, stop berating yourself for only managing to do this much at this point in time.

It is what it is. This moment is enough.

Evolving

What lies behind us and

what lies before us are tiny matters compared to what lies within us.

Oliver Wendell Holmes

Evolving As An Empath

Being labeled as 'too sensitive for your own good' or mocked for needing alone time can intimidate some of the most aware amongst human beings. Understanding how heightened sensitivities are determined by many factors such as genetics, environment, early life connections, nurturing and adverse events can help the empath to self-acceptance and to build a happy, healthy and thriving life.

All individuals need to feel safe, accepted, loved and respected, no matter their physical appearance, social status or accomplishments.

For the empath to evolve, they need to embrace their connection with emotions and energy, their ability to sense what other people cannot, protect themselves from known triggers and predators, and strengthen their belief in their own abilities and significance.

Evolving comes from the Latin word 'evolver' (to unroll) and it means to 'develop gradually', or to change over time. Evolving as a person includes constant growth to reach your full potential as a human being with an emphasis on self-realization.

It is not a one-step process or a short-term project to plan and execute, it is a way of life, constantly evolving into a better version of yourself. This may sound counterintuitive to living in the moment, however, being present means accepting what is and appreciating it, whilst striving to grow in whatever direction is needed.

'You cannot go on indefinitely being just an ordinary, decent egg. You must be hatched, or go bad'
C.S. Lewis

For the empath to evolve, they need to

- Embrace their gifts, and understand that it is not a burden but a wonderful contribution to make the world a kinder place for all
- Find self-acceptance, and develop a strong core of identity, underscored by resilience, hope and optimism
- Share their empathic gifts in their relationships, be that at home, with friends, at work, when meeting strangers in need of help
- Practice self-care, diligently and with love, to strengthen and protect themselves
- Be authentic and direct
- Have integrity
- Practice self-compassion
- Adhere to boundaries
- Allow themselves the time to recharge.

- Accept their own idiosyncrasies and work on their weaknesses
- Practice gratitude
- Grow outside their comfort zone
- Learn how to thrive

But how do you move outside your comfort zones to grow as a person so you can lead a full, rich life?

Grow Outside Your Comfort Zone

Continuous growth takes a dogged determination and tenacity, it is not about the grand gestures, such as extreme fitness programmes or visiting a diet farm, but making small changes every day to move towards a healthy, fulfilling life.

It may be something as simple as drinking an extra cup of water or saying no to one request, but eventually, it will build up into a habit and then become second nature.

Small victories empower and reengergise anyone struggling to move forward. Slay the dragons that are holding you back one tiny change at a time.

What a man can be, he must be.
This need we call self-actualisation.
Abraham Maslow

Maslow believed that all people have an inborn need for self-actualization that is the need to be all they can be. He postulated that in order to achieve these goals, one had to fulfill 'lower order' needs first, such as food, safety, love, and self-esteem.

These five needs have stood the test of time, even though many believe them not be met in hierarchical order, but to be present at all times.

Thus, self-actualizing individuals are:

- Concerned with personal growth

- Self-aware
- Less concerned with other's opinions
- Trying to fulfill their potential

Personal Effectiveness

Personal effectiveness includes using all the resources at your disposal (energy, time, talents, etc.) in all spheres of life (personal, work) to achieve your goals and master your life.

Increasing personal effectiveness involves:

- Identifying what you really want from life, what are the things that bring you true satisfaction and a sense of fulfillment and happiness
- Identifying your values and beliefs – values are deep-rooted beliefs that guide your everyday thinking and actions. They give you a clearer sense of self, helps you focus and thus provides energy to do the things that really matter and become more effective. Making sure you honor

your own beliefs, and not those of friends or what you think is expected of you helps you build authenticity. Pretending to be someone other than who you really are is exhausting and you are most likely going to be found out as a fraud or a wimp whom just follows the today crowd.

- Allowing yourself to follow your dreams is the ultimate gift you can give yourself, doing what really makes you happy and content.

- Eliminating distorted thinking can be a tall order, and sometimes you need to seek professional help with a counsellor or coach, to help you eliminate your distorted thinking about who you are, how you think, believe and act, by reflecting it back to you, so you can observe your distorted thinking objectively and find your real truth.

- Setting goals and working to achieve them – if you do not set goals you cannot stretch yourself to grow and become more effective, you will meander along disparate roads and plod through life wondering what happened. Set attainable goals, don't build castles in the sky, and work at achieving them, always stretching a bit further.

- Prioritizing the most important things in life, in your life, is a key step to evolving. Follow the things that matter, spend your precious time and effort on your priorities. Eliminate clutter and emotional baggage and let go of ideas, things and people that do not contribute to making your life better.

- Developing self-confidence, creativity, persistence and problem-solving skills – spending time improving your cognitive and emotional skills every day is an investment in the future. Read as much as you can, broaden your mind, play mind-building games and have challenging and deep conversations with family and friends. Enroll for a course in something you love, or volunteer to teach others.

- Streamlining your inner and outer images – to live an authentic life you cannot pretend to be one person and actually be another, or as some people are wont to do, be different people for different people based on what they think is expected. It is exhausting, dishonest, stressful and disastrous for your mental health. Accept yourself for who you are, and live an authentic life

- Getting organized can sound incredibly mundane and boring, but some basic organization can bring stability and peace to your life. Clear out clutter (nothing worse for making you feel crowded), find a place for everything, roughly plan your time according to priorities set, and allow for mishaps and emergencies and makes sure everyone does their fair share.

- Getting feedback as often as possible, in order to reflect and reevaluate where we are on our journey can be very useful. We are not aware of what we don't know, and if we open up to constructive feedback we may discover new ways of doing things or new strengths to develop.

- Open yourself up to learning as much as possible – stretch yourself
- Be willing to feel awkward or uncomfortable when you try something new
- Stretch your mind by reading a lot to understand world events, how people think and behave.
- Question your own thinking and behaviour patterns, understanding why you do things will help you to work on strengths and eliminate weaknesses
- Learn from people that know more
- Share your thought processes with your closest allies
- Ask for help if you are struggling
- Go out and meet new people
- Learn to walk away from negativity
- Try to understand why things are done in a certain way
- Travel if you can

- Try new things, no matter how scary or ridiculous they may be, for example
- Go ski-diving
- Watch a soap opera (if you have never done that before)
- Talk to someone you would not normally approach at a function
- Eat at a different restaurant
- Read a comic book
- Learn about different religions
- Go skinny-dipping at night
- Learn to steer clear of instant gratification, work on the long game
- Get up and try again if you fail at something or revert to old habits
- Develop persistence – keep at growing slowly, quietly, persistently.
- Integrate new habits into the fabric of your life.
- Remember, the magic happens outside your comfort zone

Venture outside your comfort zone. To stop growing is to stop living.

Robin Roberts

Image from quotefancy.com

Conclusion

Being an empath is about accepting your gifts of expanded sensitivity, living your best life and using your talents to help others understand their emotions so they can heal.

However, it is not easy living with so much emotion and energy, and often being overwhelmed due to bucket loads of jarring sensory inputs. Holding on to negativity, anger, frustration, pain, and sadness on behalf of another can be debilitating.

The empath owes it to themselves, and their loved ones, to get a clear understanding of their gifts, talents and needs, and to learn to communicate these.

As not all empaths are the same, their level of empathy may vary, their expression of their gifts may assist or bewilder others and their periods of withdrawal may debilitate relationships, friendships and make loved ones seriously question their sanity. Emotional lability is a constant companion and not always invited or wanted.

Having looked at the reasons for empaths feeling so much, the origins of these abilities and the downfalls of being an empath, it is clear that a deeper understanding is required, from both the empath and their communities.

Using the four R's to modulate their swings – reevaluate, recognize, resilience, and reverse – the empath can build a strong resistance to the pitfalls of being too open and available and avoid the nightmarish symbiotic pairing up with emotional vampires and the dark triad personalities.

By applying themselves diligently to small daily steps they can evolve and thrive by living healthy happy lives.

References

1. Dissociation of Cognitive and Emotional Empathy: The Multifaceted Empathy Test for Children and Adolescents: MET-J. al, L. Poustka et. 2010.

2.Bérangère Thirioux, François Birault and Nematollah Jaafari. Empathy Is a Protective Factor of Burnout in Physicians: New Neuro-Phenomenological Hypotheses Regarding Empathy and Sympathy in Care Relationship.

3.Zahavi, D. Simulation, projection, and empathy. . 2008, S. 514–522.

4.Damasio, A., and Carvalho, G. B. The nature of feelings: evolutionary and neurobiological origins. Nat. Rev. Neurosci. 2013, Bd. 14, S. 143–152.

5.Blanke, O. Multisensory brain mechanisms of bodily self-consciousness. . Nat. Rev. Neurosci. 13, 2012, S. 556–571.

6.Thirioux, B. Perception et apperception dans l'empathie: une critique des neurons miroir, in Les Paradoxes de l'Empathie. [Hrsg.] and A. Cuckiers eds

P. Attigui. Paris: CNRS Editions. 2011, S. 73–94.

7.The cognitive and neural time course of empathy and sympathy: an electrical neuroimaging study on self-other interaction. Thirioux, B., Mercier, M. R., Blanke, O., and Berthoz, A. 2014, Neuroscience , S. 286–306.

8.Goleman, Daniel. Empathy.

9.William A. Gentry, Todd J. Weber, and Golnaz Sadri. White Paper: Empathy in the Workplace. A Tool for Effective Leadership. s.l. : Center for Creative Leadership.

10.The Empathy Effect. Helen Riess, MD.

11.Interventions to cultivate physician empathy: a. al, Kelm et. 2014, BMC Medical Education, Bd. 14, S. 219.

12.Therapeutic empathy: what it is and what it isn't. al, Howick J. et. 2018, Journal of the Royal Society of Medicine, Bd. 111(7), S. 233-236.

13.What Does Empathy Contribute in This Age of Science and Technology? Suzanne M. Olbricht, MD.

2, August 2015, Cutis, Bd. 96, S. 78-79.

14.Weiner, Irving B. und Craighead, W. Edward. The Corsini Encyclopedia of Psychology. s.l. : John Wiley & Sons., 2010. S. 810. ISBN 978-0-470-17026-7..

15.Goleman, Daniel. Focus. The Hidden Driver of Excellence. 2013.

16.The Tao of Doing Good. Navigating between anger and acceptance in solving social issues. Allyn, David. s.l. : Stanford Social Innovation Review, 2012.

17.Who Cares? Revisiting Empathy in Asperger Syndrome. Rogers K, Dziobek I, Hassenstab J, Wolf OT, Convit A. 2007, J Autism Dev Disord, S. 709-715.

18.Neurogenetic variations in norepinephrine availability enhance perceptual vividness. Todd, Rebecca M. und al., et. 2015, Journal of Neuroscience.

19.Epistasis between 5-HTTLPR and ADRA2B polymorphisms influences attentional bias for emotional information in healthy volunteers. Naudts, Kris H., et al. 2012, International Journal of Neurospycholpharmacology.

20. Hatfield, E., Cacioppo, J. T. and Rapson, R. L. Emotional contagion. . Cambridge: : Cambridge University Press., 1994.

21. NIH.

22. Lacobani, M. Mirroring people: the science of empathy and how we connect with others. . New York: : Farrar, Straus, and Giroux., 2008.

23. Journal of Neuroscience.

24. The Science Behind Empathy and Empaths. MD, Judith Orloff. 2017, Psychology Today.

25. Super Empaths are Real.

26. Empathy hurts: Compassion for another increases both sensory and affective components of pain perception . Marco Loggia (Harvard) Jeffrey S Mogil, Mary Catherine Bushnell (NIH).

27. The fear factor: how one emotion connects altruists, psychopaths & everyone in between. . Marsh, A. New York: : Basic Books., 2017.

28. New-research-may-support-the-existence-of-empaths.

29.Dissociation of Cognitive and Emotional Empathy: The Multifaceted Empathy Test for Children and Adolescents.

30.Effect_of_visual_stimuli_of_pain_on_empathy_ brain_network_in_people_with_and_without_Autis m_Spectrum_Disorder.

31.Five-Factor Model of Personality. Christopher J. Soto, Joshua J. Jackson. 2018, OxfordBibliographies.

32.Measuring Individual Differences in Empathy: Evidence for a Multidimensional Approach. Davis, Mark H. 1, 1983, Journal of Personality and Social Psychology., Bd. 44, S. 113–26. .

33.The Empath's Survival Guide. Orloff, Dr. Judith.

34.The "false consensus effect": An egocentric bias in social perception and attribution processes. Lee Ross, David Greene, Pamela House. 1977, Semantic Scholar.

35.Does_Feeling_Empathy_Lead_to_Compassion_F atigue_or_Compassion_Satisfaction_The_Role_of_ Time_Perspective.

36.Neural Responses to Ingroup and Outgroup

Members' Suffering Predict Individual Differences in Costly Helping". . Hein, Grit, et al. 1, 2010, Neuron, Bd. 68, S. 149–160.

37.Emotional Vampires: People who Drain you Dry. PhD, Albert Bernstein. 2012.

38.The Six Pillars of Self-esteem: the definitive work on self-esteem by the leading pioneer in the field. Branden, Nathaniel. 1995.

39.The Subtle Art of not Giving a F*ck. Manson, Mark.

40.Maslach Burnout Inventory Manual. ResearchGate.

41.Empathy at the Heart of Darkness: Empathy deficits that bind the dark triad and those that mediate indirect relational aggression. Heym, Nadja et al. 2019, Frontiers in Psychiatry.

42.Jones, D. N., Paulhus, D. L. Differentiating the dark triad within the interpersonal circumplex. [Hrsg.] L. M. Horowitz und S. N. Strack. Handbook of interpersonal theory and research. New York: Guilford, 2010, S. 249-67.

43.An Examination of the Dark Triad Constructs with Regard to Prosocial Behavior. Tackett, Jack A Palmer and Seth. 5, 2018, Acta Psychopathologica, Bd. 4.

44. Do I win, does the company win, or do we both win? Moderate traits of the Dark Triad and profit maximization. Marcia Figueredo D'Souza, et al. 4, 2019, Revista Contabilidade & Finanças, Bd. 79.

45.Sensory Processing Sensitivity: A review in the light of the evolution of biological responsivity. Elaine N. Aron, Arthur Aron and Jadzia Jagiellowicz. X, 2012, Personality and Social Psychology Review, Bd. XX, S. 1-21.

46.Sensory Processing Sensitivity in the Context of Environmental Sensitivity: A Critical Review and Development of Research Agenda. al, Corina U. Grven et. 2018, Preprints 2018.

47.The Highly Sensitive Person: How to Thrive when the World Overwhelms You. Elaine N. Arn, Ph.D.

48.Differential susceptibility to the environment: An evolutionary -neurodevelopment theory. al, Bruce J. Ellis et. 2011, Development and Psychopathology, Bd.

23, S. 7-28.

49.Social Anxiety Disorder: more then just shyness. NIH: National Institute of Mental Health.

50.Bipolar Disorder. NIH: National Institute of Mental Health.

51.The balance between feeling and knowing: affective and cognitive empathy are reflected in the brain's intrinsic functional dynamics. al, Cox CL et. 6, 2012, Soc Cogn Affect Neurosci , Bd. 7, S. 727-37.

52.Borderline Personality Disorder. NIH: National Institute of Mental Health.

53.Leadership Vitality. Ehlers, W.

54.Resilience. Psychology Today.

55. Food for Mood: Relevance of Nutritional Omega-3 Fatty Acids for Depression and Anxiety. Laye, Thomas Larrieu and Sophie. 2018, Frontiers in Psychology, Bd. 9, S. 1047.

56.I know how you feel: the warm-altruistic personality profile and the empathic brain. Haas, BW, et al. 3, 2015, PLOS ONE. , Bd. 10, S. e0120639.

Disclaimer

The information contained in this book and its components, is meant to serve as a comprehensive collection of strategies that the author of this book has done research about. Summaries, strategies, tips and tricks are only recommendations by the author, and reading this book will not guarantee that one's results will exactly mirror the author's results.

The author of this book has made all reasonable efforts to provide current and accurate information for the readers of this book. The author and its associates will not be held liable for any unintentional errors or omissions that may be found.

The material in the book may include information by third parties. Third party materials comprise of opinions expressed by their owners. As such, the author of this book does not assume responsibility or liability for any third party material or opinions.

written expressed and signed permission from the author.

Printed in Great Britain
by Amazon